TRACKING TALENTS

TRACKING TALENTS

for the identification of multiple talents

Françoys Gagné, Ph.D.

Department of Psychology
Université du Québec à Montréal

Prufrock Press, Inc.
P.O. Box 8813
Waco, Texas 76714-8813
(800) 998-2208
FAX (800) 240-0333
http://www.prufrock.com / Prufrock@prufrock.com

Table of Contents

Acknowledgements

* *

Tracking Talents is the end-product of a five-year research project, named "Project PAIRS," (French for *peers*). It was made possible thanks to a generous three-year grant from the "Fonds FCAR," the scientific research grant-giving agency within the Quebec Ministry of Education. As director of Project PAIRS, I am pleased to express my gratitude for their important financial help.

Many students and research assistants participated in this project, some of them using parts of the data collected to write their master's thesis. Among members of my research laboratory, called the "Groupe d'Intervention et de Recherche en Douance et Talent - GIREDT" (Group for Intervention and Research on Giftedness and Talent), three played a major role in the realization of this research project. M. Jean Bégin, now a Ph.D. in psychology, supervised the statistical methodology for the psychometric data analyses. M. Denis Godbout, now a Ph.D. in psychology, was in charge of the logistics for the two major data collections in over 350 classrooms in the Greater Montreal area. Ms. Lise Talbot did most of the computer work for the data analyses of the students' answers. Without their dedicated work, this project would not have succeeded as it did.

Finally, Dr. Sandra I. Kay, district coordinator of gifted and talented programs for Monroe-Woodbury Central Schools (NY), deserves special thanks; not only did she supervise a tryout of the final forms and collect precious feedback from the participating teachers, but she also read the revised draft of this manual and offered very useful comments.

Now that Project PAIRS is coming to its close with the completion of the final forms and of this User's Manual, it is my hope that these instruments—even in their unfinished state, psychometrically speaking—will help professionals and teachers in their efforts to identify among students those who show promise in various fields of human activity.

Françoys Gagné, Ph. D.
January 1999

To my mother "Deleine,"
a woman without peers,
whose selfless love
and countless sacrifices
are engraved forever
in my heart.

Chapter One

❖ ❖

Rationale and Overview

The purpose of the *Tracking Talents* nomination forms is to gather information from **multiple sources** about **multiple abilities**. The multiple sources are the students themselves, their peers in the same classroom or grade, and their teacher(s). This is why *Tracking Talents* is described as Peer, Teacher, and Self-Nomination Forms (or PTSNFs). The multiple abilities include not only the usual cognitive abilities and academic talents, but social and physical abilities, as well as technological and artistic talents. This first chapter briefly surveys problems related to the identification of gifts and talents, focusing on the more immediately relevant questions of content and sources. It then describes the specific contents and structure of the *Tracking Talents* PTSNFs.

A - Beyond IGAT: Multiple Abilities

The concepts of giftedness and talent have traditionally been defined in terms of either cognitive or academic abilities. Cognitive abilities are best measured by IQ tests, whereas teacher-made or standardized achievement tests typically assess academic abilities. In one of the most comprehensive surveys of identification practices in the U.S., Cox, Daniel, and Boston (1985) confirmed that group IQ tests and achievement tests were used in over 90% of the school districts as preferred means of identification. These observations brought this author to describe as IGAT (Intellectually Gifted and Academically Talented) the typical students served by most American school-based enrichment services (Gagné, 1995b).

While these identification practices remain by far the most typical, some school districts have begun exploring a much larger spectrum of abilities, especially in arts and technology. Proposals for such a broadened view of giftedness and talent are by no means recent. For instance, De Haan and Havigurst (1957) proposed a definition of giftedness that specified six domains of excellence: intellectual ability, creative thinking, scientific ability, social leadership, mechanical skills, and talents in the fine arts. It was followed by the famous "Marland definition" (1972), which also listed multiple abilities:

> Children capable of high performance include those with demonstrated achievement and/or potential ability in any of the following areas, singly or in combination: 1. general intellectual ability, 2. specific academic aptitude, 3. creative or productive thinking, 4. leadership ability, 5. visual and performing arts, 6. psychomotor ability. (p. 5)

A decade later, Gardner's (1983) theory of multiple intelligences opened the inventory of abilities a bit more with his proposal of seven basic "intelligences." They were named linguistic, musical, logical-mathematical, spatial, bodily-kinesthetic, intrapersonal, and interpersonal. To each of these intelligences corresponds a particular type of giftedness. That theory was soon followed by our own *Differentiated Model of Giftedness and Talent* (Gagné, 1985; see also 1993a, 1995b), which proposed five domains of natural abilities or gifts (cognitive, creative, socioaffective, physical, and "others"), as well as numerous fields of talent, covering all areas of human activity. Those not familiar with that theory will find in Appendix A a brief overview of the DMGT. The DMGT directly inspired the planning of Project PAIRS, especially its goal of covering as large a spectrum of human abilities as could be reliably assessed among students.

B - Beyond Testing: Multiple Sources

Abilities are best measured in well-standardized situations. There is no doubt in our mind that a good IQ test easily beats any form of subjective assessment, even from the keenest observers. But, as we open the field of abilities to be assessed, multiple assessments soon lose any practical feasibility. This is where judges find their usefulness. Gathering evaluative judgments about self or other people's abilities requires much less effort, and many abilities can be assessed in a short amount of time. But, every procedural decision implies some trade-off. In the present case, we trade breadth for depth. On the one hand, we have to accept the reduced precision of subjective judgments; on the other, we take advantage of the procedural simplicity. The *Tracking Talents* nomination forms make it possible to gather information from three different sources: peers, teachers, and the students themselves. Let us examine more closely each of these sources.

1. Peer nominations

As the name Project PAIRS emphasized, the experimental forms of *Tracking Talents* were initially designed to be used as peer nomination forms (PNF) only. These questionnaires have been popular as screening instruments for abilities at least since the early '30s (Gagné, 1989). All PNFs differ from sociometric questionnaires in a major way. Sociometric questionnaires ask students about those with whom they would like (or not like) to work, play, take a trip, and so forth; their subject is social attraction (or rejection). On the other hand, peer nomination forms ask students to act as judges or observers of other students' behavior, and report their judgment about that behavior: it is no longer social *attraction*, but social *perception*. Students can be asked to identify those who act more agressively, show more shyness, or exhibit special abilities. This last purpose characterizes the **Tracking Talents** nomination forms.

One of the major advantages of PNFs is the ease with which they can be written, administered, and compiled; there is also the advantage of the large number of judges contributing their information to the group judgment. Psychometricians, the professionals who create tests and questionnaires, know very well the power of large numbers; this is why they prefer longer exams to shorter ones. Even if the judges are young and less mature than teachers, they can be in a good position to assess some abilities that do not show themselves as clearly to teachers (e.g., physical or social abilities). Moreover, although a student's individual judgment is less accurate than that of the average teacher, the fact that the resulting score will come from the addition of 30 or so student judgments tends to reduce significantly the subjectivity inherent in each of them. This is why peer nominations were mentioned by at least 25% of the school administrators who completed the national survey mentioned earlier (Cox, Daniel, & Boston, 1985).

The quasi-totality of PNFs used in U.S. school districts are *not* psychometric instruments; they were not created by professional test writers, nor were they submitted to a rigorous examination of their technical qualities, especially their reliability and validity. Only one instrument, the Muffs (Delisle, Gubbins, Ciabotti, Salvatore, & Rucker, 1984), has been offered commercially, and it can be criticized on a number of grounds (Gagné, 1989).

2. Teacher nominations

Teacher nominations are among the most popular identification techniques. The practice of using them as sources of nominations probably goes as far back as the first searches for academically promising students. Terman (1925) used teacher nominations extensively to create a limited pool of candidates in his search for the intellectually gifted students of his famous longitudinal study. Teacher nominations can take many forms, from a simple list of the names of the gifted students in the classroom, without even a description of what gifted means, to detailed checklists of behavioral characteristics. Every handbook in gifted education discusses the pros and cons of teacher identification (e.g., Borland, 1989; Clark, 1996; Davis & Rimm, 1989; Gallagher, 1985).

The value of teacher nominations has been the subject of many studies, some of them very critical. In one of the most frequently cited studies (Pegnato & Birch, 1959), the authors criticized them because of the large percentage of intellectually gifted students that were left unnamed. These students were found to have IQ scores well above the threshold required to be labeled gifted, usually between 125 and 130. But, most of these studies were later themselves criticized for their methodological limits (Gagné, 1994; Hoge & Cudmore, 1986). Nowadays, there appears to be a general consensus that when teachers are well-trained concerning what they should look for when asked to identify intellectually gifted students, their effectiveness will be quite satisfactory.

Teacher nominations have one major drawback, namely the fact that the information comes from a single judge or observer. This is just the opposite of the main advantage mentioned for peer nominations. One might argue that teachers are much better observers of behavior than their students, which is probably true of the typical teacher as compared to the typical elementary-school student. Still, the fact that there is only one judgment, as compared

5

to 30 or so in the case of peers, significantly reduces the reliability of that information. Thus, logic and common sense suggest that, on average, peer scores should be more reliable than teacher scores, if only because of the large number of judges with which these peer scores are computed. This was confirmed in our own study (see chapter 5, part D.4).

3. Self-nominations

Gathering self-nominations is easy. It can be done by asking individual students to point out, among a group of items, those for which they perceive themselves to be among the top two (or three, or four) in their group. Another simple way to obtain self-nominations is to allow students to name themselves as part of the process of gathering peer nominations in a whole group. Massé (1992) did her master's thesis on the problem of self-nominations. Her search for relevant literature on that subject revealed little systematic use of self-nominations as a source of information for the identification of gifted and talented students.

Yet, that approach remains very popular, since a majority of special schools request interested youngsters to submit an application, a form of self-nomination, as the first step in their selection process. Uses of self-evaluations in other contexts (e.g., personality assessment) have shown that they have undeniable value as well as limits. Massé (see Massé & Gagné, 1996) examined the problem of bias, which was considered a definite risk by the Project PAIRS team in view of the students' young age. She found that students had indeed overly positive views of their abilities, naming themselves much more frequently than they were named by peers or teachers. On the other hand, these judgments remained moderately correlated with peer and teacher judgments. The fact that self-nominations do not decrease the reliability of other information, added to the fact that students insist that they be allowed to nominate themselves, led us to include them as part of the peer nomination process. The problems associated with their use will be discussed in more detail in chapter 4 (see part D.1).

In conclusion, as with any other form of psychological assessment, the use of judges has advantages and disadvantages. Potential users should be aware of these limitations when they decide to adopt that technique.

C - Overview of Tracking Talents

This overview briefly describes the content and format of the **Tracking Talents** PTSNFs. It also explains in which educational contexts these forms will be most useful.

1. What they are

Most nomination forms focus on intellectual abilities, and will usually contain just a few questions, sometimes only one. The **Tracking Talents** PTSNFs have been created to assess many more abilities beyond intellectual ones.

a. *The two forms.* **Tracking Talents** exists in two forms: A and B. Each form is composed of 12 items. As shown in Table 1, the items cover not only intellectual abilities and academic talents, but abilities in the fields of technology, arts, sports, and social skills. These judgments by students will produce not only a general "giftedness" score, but also scores for individual items as well as groups of items. There are at least two items for each ability domain, and there is no overlap between the two forms. These two sets of 12 items were chosen at the end of the research project as the best group of items to represent the diversity of students' abilities as they seem to manifest themselves in the school environnement, at least in terms of being easy enough to assess by peers, as well as teachers.

Table 1
Grouping of Items in Forms A and B

Form A	**Form B**
Academic talent	**Physical abilities**
1. Encyclopedia (general knowledge)	**1.** Hercules (strength)
6. Lightning (fast to answer questions)	**8.** Tireless one (endurance)
7. Scientist	**12.** Hare (speed)
12. Bright idea (original, creative)	
Mechanical/Technical talent	**Arts (music)**
2. Handyman	**2.** Musician
4. Programmer	**5.** Singer
10. Mechanic	**10.** Dancer
Arts (drama)	**Arts (visual)**
3. Comedian	**4.** Artist
9. Actor	**9.** Craftsperson
Interpersonal abilities	**Interpersonal abilities**
(ethical / affective)	(social influence)
5. Counselor	**3.** Leader
8. Stimulator	**6.** Sociable
11. Judge	**7.** Spokesperson
	11. Speaker

---

b. *The items.* Figure 1 on page 8 shows a typical item from **Tracking Talents**. Each item is composed of four elements: (1) an *icon* that illustrates the subject of the item and acts as an attraction point for students; (2) a *title* that specifies the type of talent being sought; (3) a behavioral *description* of that talent; and (4) three *circles* in which are placed the students' choices. With only a few exceptions (e.g., Handyman, Hercules), titles are gender neutral. Moreover, to reduce sexual bias toward boys, all descriptions begin as follows: "A [title] is a girl or a boy who ..."

Figure 1
Item Format in Tracking Talents

COMEDIAN
A comedian is a girl or a boy who makes
everyone laugh with her or his jokes,
imitations or improvisations.

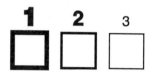

---

c. *The task.* Students are asked to provide three *ranked* choices for each of the items. This number was empirically proven to be quite sufficient to provide reliable talent scores (see chapter 5, part C.1). Moreover, since regular groups usually comprise between 25 and 30 students, that number of choices corresponds to a selection ratio of 10% to 12%, which is considered a middle-of-the-road position—and our own personal choice of threshold (Gagné, 1998)—to determine how many should be considered gifted or talented.

Asking students to write up to 36 full names would have made the task very time-consuming; the scoring would also have become a tedious process. This is why we adopted a more efficient technique, based on an alphabetically ordered list of the students in the class, numbered from 1 to N. When students choose a peer, they must find that peer's name in the list, note the corresponding number, and put that number in the appropriate circle provided at the right of the item's description. The three circles have been drawn with decreasing density to highlight the decreasing importance of the rankings.

It takes approximately 20 to 30 minutes to complete either form of *Tracking Talents*, even less the second time around when both forms are used. During the research phase, this duration was shown to be short enough to maintain students' interest in the task, thus minimizing random answers due to boredom. In the language of psychometrics, random answers correspond to measurement error, something to avoid as much as possible because it reduces the reliability of the information.

2. When to use them

a. *Talent development screening.* **Tracking Talents** was created first and foremost to be part of a battery of instruments designed to screen talented students for the purpose of offering them appropriate enrichment services. While this is not the place to tackle the complex problem of screening and identification in the field of gifted education, one comment seems worth mentioning. **Tracking Talents** is based on subjective human judgments instead of more objective measures of abilities; consequently, it should never be used alone for identification purposes. Its information needs to be buttressed with "stronger" sources of information, for instance, IQ tests, standardized achievement tests, tests of musical or physical aptitudes, measured performances in sports, portfolios of past achievements in arts, and so forth.

b. *Other uses.* Another appropriate reason to use this instrument could be to increase the teachers' knowledge of their students. Indeed, during the research and tryout phases, we found that the teachers were often very surprised and excited by the **Tracking Talents** results, finding much to learn from the discrepancies between their own choices and those of peer and self-nominations. The scores made them aware of new and broader ways to look at their students' abilities and strengths; the concept of talent took a new meaning as academic achievement was shown to be only one among many forms of talent. Teachers found that knowledge not only interesting in itself, but also potentially useful for curricular purposes. Some of these uses are described in chapter 4, part D.

3. Conditions of use to watch for

Empirical tryouts have shown that there are some best and less-than-best conditions for the use of the **Tracking Talents** PTSNFs. They concern the minimum and maximum grade levels that are appropriate for their use as a peer-self nomination form, as well as a few other considerations.

a. *Minimum grade level.* When these questionnaires are used for peer or self-nominations, our research has shown that they can be presented to groups of students *from grade 4 up*. We did not try the forms in lower grades because we thought that the language level might be too advanced. Also, we feared that the answering procedure, namely finding the chosen student in an alphabetical list, might be difficult for too many younger students. Still, teachers who believe that most of their third-graders could complete the task without much difficulty should not hesitate to use **Tracking Talents**.

b. *Maximum grade level.* There are two distinct problems associated with the use of **Tracking Talents** with older students, especially with high school groups. First and foremost, nominations become difficult when students are together only part of the day due to group composition changes for each subject matter. At that point, there are too many students within any particular group who are not well-known by their peers, and that increases the risk of random choices. Indeed, our tryouts have shown that the students themselves often refuse to do the task for that particular reason. This is why we recommend that these forms be used only with *stable groups*, groups who remain together most of the time during the week. Second, the wording of the items is targeted at younger students; with older ones, **Tracking Talents** might have a problem of "*face validity*," as older students judge the language too babyish! Our experience indicates that these two problems do not appear until grades 8 or 9.

c. *Class size.* Because the scores correspond to the aggregation of many individual choices, it is recommended that **Tracking Talents** be used with groups of at least 15 students, and, preferably, 20 students or more.

d. *Valid teacher nominations*. When **Tracking Talents** is used as a teacher nomination form, only those teachers who know that group of students very well should be invited to complete a nomination form. This is not a major problem, since specialist teachers who see many groups of students weekly (e.g., arts, physical education) will frequently refuse to complete these forms, stating their lack of sufficient knowledge of the students being assessed.

While it is true that most specialist teachers do not possess as broad a knowledge of students as regular classroom teachers who spend much more time with them, they have acquired *in their own field* precious information that should be tapped if it is relevant to the screening purposes. For example, music teachers could be invited to submit their own nominations for the Musical subgroup in Form B (see Table 1), physical education teachers could be invited to propose their choices for the Physical subgroup, also in Form B, and so forth. These specialist teachers should also be invited to complete other items in a form if they feel that they possess adequate information (e.g., about some socioaffective abilities, like leadership abilities).

Chapter Two

❖ ❖

Administering Tracking Talents

A s you will see in this chapter, *Tracking Talents* is very easy to administer. Still, to ensure well-controlled testing conditions, it is recommended that examiners who have no testing experience receive some minimal training.

A - General Considerations

Here are some situations that can have a significant impact on the quality of the scores derived from the peer nominations. Please examine them carefully.

a. *Appropriate time frame.* When should teachers administer *Tracking Talents* in their classroom? One might think it is better to wait toward the end of the school year, so that the students will have had more time to get to know each other well. But, usually, these students will have been in the same school since kindergarten or first grade; in small schools, they might even have stayed together as a group since their first year in school. In such cases, administering *Tracking Talents* close to the beginning of the school year would probably not affect the results in any significant way. Choosing the appropriate time is a matter of judgment about the degree of knowledge students have of each other; the better they know each other, the more reliable the results will be.

b. *Which form to use.* The contents of Table 1 should facilitate the choice of the form that will be best tailored to the purposes of the identification process. Usually, when the time comes to choose the identification instruments, an enrichment service has already been planned, and the characteristics of its target population have been identified. This planning indicates which abilities in either Forms A or B are of special interest in that context. In some special situations, a program coordinator might want to use both forms. This poses no problem; but, a one-week interval is recommended between both administrations.

c. *Sensitizing the students.* There is no rule against showing the **Tracking Talents** booklets to the students some days or weeks prior to administering the nomination form. In fact, it might make the students look at their peers more closely to detect who among them would be the best performers for each of the abilities described in the form that will be used.

d. *Newly arrived students.* The presence of newly arrived students in a group creates a potential problem, not only because they might not be well-known by their peers, thus receiving from them few choices, but also because they may have some difficulty identifying the more able in the various fields. If they try to answer with their limited knowledge, they will introduce measurement error. If there is only one such new student in a group, that error will be negligible. The impact might become significant if there are three or four of these students. In that case, it would be wise to put a mark on their copy; you will be invited to check during scoring whether their answers diverge significantly or not from those of the other students.

e. *Gender distribution.* One of our studies (see chapter 5, part D.5) has clearly shown that boys tend to choose boys, while girls tend to choose girls. In other words, there is a clear gender bias, if not a major one. This is understandable since boys and girls do not mix much at these ages, either in the classroom or in the school yard. Thus, members of each gender probably know better the abilities of their same-sex peers, and will tend to look in that direction when searching for the best performers in a given domain. When both genders are about equally represented, which is fortunately the case in most classrooms, this bias will cancel itself out. But, when there is a large majority of students of one gender, there is a definite risk that those in the "gender minority" will not appear as often as they should among the more able in any area. What can be done about that? We have no specific solution to offer, except to make you aware of the fact and its impact on the validity of the talent scores. To our knowledge, there is no simple way to compensate for that bias.

B - Preparation

Copies of **Tracking Talents** are not reusable. Check that you have at least one for every student in the group, plus one for the teacher (if included in the data collection).

Prepare in advance the numbered and alphabetically ordered class list(s), placing surnames first, in capital letters so their order will be easily seen, and adding first names with the first letter only in capitals (see Figure 2 on page 13). Precede each name with a very legible number (see next page); that number will be called henceforth *Student Identification Number (SIN)*. It should be easy to list all students in the group, using only one column, on a single letter-size sheet of paper.

Figure 2
Recommended Format for Class List

SIN	Name
1.	BABEL, Tower
2.	CAPITAL, Letter
3.	CUSTER, General
... and so forth...	
27.	TONGUE, Incheek
28.	WISHFUL, Thinking

Note: Students who are absent from school on the day the questionnaire is administered *should be* in the class list: they have as much right to be named as those who are present.

C - Directions

First, distribute the materials: (a) a copy of the **Tracking Talents** questionnaire, and (b) the numbered class list. You are then ready to give the following directions. They should *not* be read. The essential ideas should be memorized and the teacher or other test examiner should use his or her own wording.

a. *Describing the task.* "Today, the task I will ask you to do ["the game we will play together" for the younger ones] is to find within your group those who are best at doing different things or activities, like answering questions in school, playing music, running, working with computers, being a leader, and so forth." [Try to adapt your examples to the particular form you are using.]

   "For each ability, you will have to find the *three* best students in this group, and rank them first, second, and third. You are free to choose anyone you wish, a girl or a boy. You just need to be sure that the person you choose is really the best for that ability. It is *very important* that you do not say out loud who your choices are; you must keep it to yourself. Now, let's look at the materials you will need to do this task [or play this game]."

b. *Describing the materials.* "You have been given two things. The booklet called **Tracking Talents** describes the task you will do [the game you will play]. The other sheet of paper is a list of all the students in this group, placed in alphabetical order and numbered from I to N. You will make your choices from that list. This means that you cannot choose students who are in other groups or classrooms. Is that clear? Also, who is (are) absent today? [Get students to answer.] Are they on the class list? Yes, they are there because you can name them (him or her) as anybody else.

"Now, let's look at the booklet for a few moments. The 12 abilities we will be looking for are described in the inside pages. As you can see, there is the ... [point to some of them]. You see the three little circles at the right of each item? That is where you will answer. I will show you in a minute how to do that. But, first, let's go back to the cover page and look at the questions there."

c. *Completing the cover page.* Have them complete the information on the cover page: the name of the school, the name or number of their group (e.g., 4-A, or Mary's 4th grade), their birth date, and gender. The last information requested, their SIN on the class list, is the best occasion for them to practice using the class list to find a number corresponding to a name on the list (their own), and transfer that number to the cover page. With younger students, you should stop at this point and check that each student understands that task, and has written the correct SIN. You can do that verbally without having to go through the rows. *This check is very important* since the validity of the technique depends on a perfect mastery of that task.

d. *Answering the first item.* Proceed to the first item in the form (Encyclopedia in Form A, and Hercules in Form B). Present the item as follows: "The first item is called the Encyclopedia. What is an Encyclopedia? What does the drawing show? Let's look at the description. It says that an Encyclopedia is a girl or a boy who knows lots of things about all kinds of subjects, not just school subjects. Think of who is the best Encyclopedia in your group, the student (girl or boy) who knows lots of things about all kinds of subjects, not just school subjects. *Don't say it out loud,* keep it to yourself. When you think you know who that student is, look up his or her name in the class list and note the number just beside that name. Then, put that number in the big circle at the right of the item, the one with the digit '1' above it. When you look in the list, be careful to note the correct number, the one just beside the name of the student you have chosen. Each number means a different student. If you put wrong numbers in the little circles, you will be naming the wrong persons, and nobody will know that you have made a mistake when checking out the numbers. So, take your time: finding the correct number for your choice is very important because that is where mistakes can happen. If you make a mistake, you can erase your answer and write the correct number in its place.

"When you have written the number of the student you think is the best Encyclopedia, think who is your second best choice, who is the next student, girl or boy, who knows lots of things about all kinds of subjects, not just school subjects. Again, look up his or her name on the class list and check the number beside that name. Then write that number in the circle with a '2' above it; the '2' means that it is your second choice. Finally, do the same for your third choice. Find him or her within this group, check his/her number in the class list, and write that number in the circle with a '3' above it. You have completed the first item."

e. *Forcing or not forcing?* When students say that they cannot name a peer for a given choice, the examiner should answer as follows: "If you can find the first two best, but cannot name a third choice, *do not* put any number just to fill the circle. Leave it empty. It could even happen that you are unable to identify a second choice, or even a first choice. If, after having looked closely at the names of your friends on the class list, you are still unable to name somebody, then it is better *not* to write anything in the circles."

f. *Allowing self-nominations.* The subject of self-nominations will probably have been mentioned well before this point. When students ask about naming themselves, here is what you should answer. "It will probably happen that you will think that *you* are the one who is best, or second best, or third best for a particular ability. If you are sure about that, you can write your own number in the circle. But, be careful not to name yourself too often; take time to look at the class list and think of all the students in the group. You have to be sure that there is no one else in the group who is better than you for that ability."

g. *Answering the rest of the items.* With younger students, the examiner should repeat (in shorter form) the above directions for each item. This way, most students will go through the form at the same pace. Leave ample time for them to think about their choices. Remind them regularly that they must not say out loud the names of those they have chosen, nor point them out, or look at them too insistently. If this was done too often during the administration of the questionnaire, then that "cheating" would *artificially increase* the reliability of the information. Answers would give a false impression of good agreement between the students in the group. Unfortunately, that high level of agreement would not be the result of group perceptiveness, but rather the impact of undue influence from a few students toward those who are hesitant about their choices (see chapter 4, part A, and chapter 5, part C.2).

    With older students, you can let them go at their own pace after completing the directions for the first item. Some will complete it quickly, while others will agonize over every choice.

h. *Gathering the completed copies.* Students can either bring back to the examiner their completed copy as soon as they have finished, at which point the examiner should check that the correct SIN was put on the cover page; you will need that number to identify self-nominations. One way to do it with younger students is to use alphabetical order to ask each one to bring his or her completed copy.

    As suggested at the beginning of this chapter, mark the copy of any newly arrived student so you will later be able to compare their answers to those of the rest of the group. Do the same for any student who seemed to have some difficulty understanding the task and completing the questionnaire correctly.

Chapter Three

❈ ❈

Scoring Tracking Talents

This chapter contains detailed directions for the scoring of the peer nominations. In the case of the teacher and self data, no computing is required because there is only one judge: these nominations are treated as individual data. The scoring directions are written in the form of sequential commands, as if we were speaking to the person doing the task. Aware that many professionals will do the scoring manually instead of using the available computer program, we have tried to be as user-friendly as possible. The scoring task has been subdivided into four steps:

1. verifying that the completed copies contain valid information (part A);
2. transferring the students' choices to a summary form called the Data Sheet (part B);
3. computing talent scores for each student and writing them on the Score Sheet (part C); and
4. tranferring the teacher's choices and self-nominations (part D).

> *Note:* A copy of the Data Sheet, Scoring Pad, Score Sheet Form A, and Score Sheet Form B appear in Appendix D and may be copied freely.

At the risk of being judged a bit "wordy," we decided to explain the major operations in the scoring process; we recommend that all users carefully read these explanations. Still, if some users feel that they understand the principles very well and want to skip them, they can go directly to part E, which offers a step-by-step checklist of all the scoring operations described in this chapter. But, if you have any doubt about a particular operation, do not try to guess. Come back to the proper section to verify the correct procedure.

A - Data Verification

This first step aims at deleting any copies that might contain invalid information. The first criterion is the number of choices made out of a maximum of 36 (12 items x 3 choices). During the research project, we looked at thousands of copies and found that most were at least 80% complete and that the missing answers tended to increase from the first to the last choice. In other words, it was very easy for most students to identify the most able student for any proposed ability (only 6% of missing first choices). It was a bit more difficult to find a second choice (about 17% of missing data), and still more difficult to propose a fourth choice (about 33% of missing answers). These percentages varied from item to item, some of them (e.g., Encyclopedia, Calculator, Musician) being easier to answer than others (e.g., Counselor, Dancer, Judge).

For the research database, we fixed the minimum percentage of answers in a student copy at 33% (12 answers out of the maximum of 36), judging that a lower number of answers left serious doubts as to how well these students understood the task or knew their peers' abilities. Consequently, we *strongly recommend* that you:
1. *discard* any copy with less than 12 choices overall; and
2. *put temporarily aside* the copies that you marked to identify a newly arrived student or one whose understanding of the task appeared doubtful (see chapter 2).

B - Transferring Nominations to the Data Sheet

The second step in the scoring process consists of transferring the answers (the SINs of the chosen peers) to the Data Sheet. The Data Sheet (see Figure 3) has 30 *columns*, one per respondent, plus a column at right for the teacher's nominations. A *respondent* is defined as any student who has completed a valid copy, one whose information can be transferred.

> *Note:* If your group has more than 30 respondents, you will need a second copy of the Data Sheet to transfer the additional respondents.

Look at Figure 3 from top to bottom. You will notice that the *rows* are grouped in threes: the first row of a trio is for first choices, the second row for second choices, and so forth. There are 12 groups of three rows, one group for each item; they are numbered in the left-hand margin. The bottom row will be used to write the number of self-nominations. Before going further, we need to explain briefly how the scoring works.

a. *Scoring principle.* When **Tracking Talents** is used as a peer nomination form, students' scores for a given item are based on the number of nominations received from their peers. But, we must take into consideration the *rank* of the nomination; no doubt that a first choice means, in the eyes of the nominator, a higher ability level than a second choice, and so forth. This is why a first choice is given more importance (3 points) than a second choice (2 points) or a third choice (only 1 point). To help with the scoring, the three rows for each item on the Data Sheet have been identified, at left, not with the rank of the choice, but with the *number of points* (3, 2, 1) given to these choices (see Figure 3). We will use the SUM of these points to compute a student's talent score for each ability.

b. *Transfer procedure.* First, place all the *valid* copies of a group in sequential order of SIN, with student 1 on top. If you have put aside some doubtful copies, place them underneath, also in sequential order. Then, place the teacher's completed copy (if there is one) at the bottom of the pile. You are now ready to do the transfer. Note that you will be transferring each student's choices (the SINs of his or her peers) *vertically*, from top to bottom, in the *same column*.

Figure 3
Example of a Completed Data Sheet

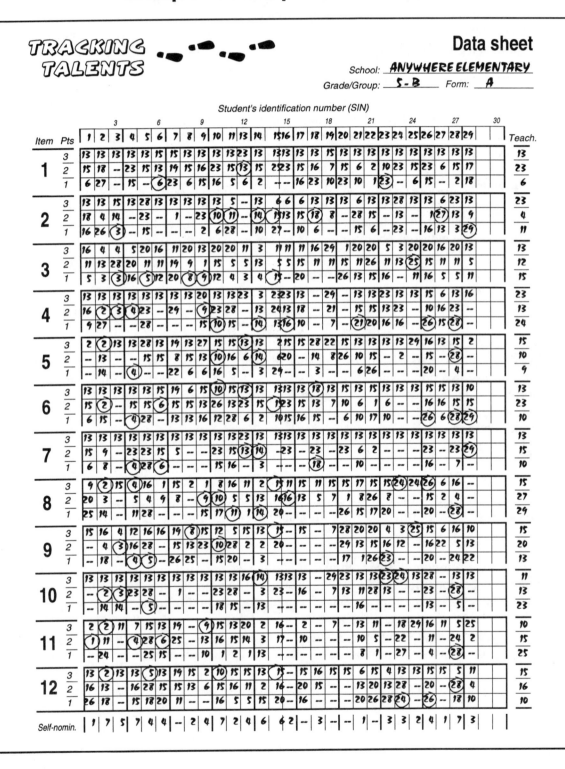

Begin your transfer in the leftmost column. Put in the top row the first respondent's SIN (usually 1), then transfer the three choices for item 1, *one under the other*. Continue down that same column with the three choices for items 2 to 12. Always place the first choice on the first of the three rows. If one of the circles is empty, put a dash (-) in the corresponding cell in the Data Sheet and move down to the next row. For example, Figure 3 shows that student 1's three choices were SINs 13, 15, and 6 in that order; note also that she made only one choice—student 2 in first rank position—for item 5, forcing us to skip two rows and go directly to the next item.

Note: The three choices of a student for each item must differ because the same peer cannot be chosen twice for the same item by the same judge! So, check for *repeats* of the same number among the three choices given. You won't find many; they are very rare. If you do find a repeat, eliminate the second (lower rank) of these repeated choices and replace it with a dash (-); it will become a missing answer.

Now, take the copy of the second student, and repeat that procedure with that second judge, placing the answers in the column *immediately to the right* of the first respondent. Do this transfer for the whole group. It should not take more than 20 to 30 minutes. Be careful to write clearly to help minimize errors in the next scoring step.

c. *Verifying the copies put aside.* [Skip this operation if no copies were put aside.] When the data from all the "regular" respondents have been transferred, take the first of the copies you temporarily put aside and compare the choices made, item by item, with those in the Data Sheet. What you are looking for is choices that are *often the same as the more popular nominations of the other students*. The pairing and the ranking need not be perfect. But, if you observe that *a majority* of that student's choices do *not* correspond to popular nominations, it is preferable to delete that copy. These "personal" nominations would not improve the talent scores of the students already chosen by many peers. Repeat that verification with the other copies left aside, deciding each time whether the choices are similar enough to those already transferred to be included with them. Remember that what you are looking for is good agreement between the judges.

d. *Teacher information.* If the teacher also completed **Tracking Talents**, you can add these choices at the right of the Data Sheet, as shown in Figure 3. At the end of that transfer operation, you will have produced a SINful Data Sheet [I couldn't resist the pun!], just like the one in Figure 3.

e. *Counting the self-nominations.* Now that you have a completed Data Sheet, one short task remains to be done: identifying the self-nominations. In the leftmost column, check the respondent's SIN at the top, then mark (by circling or highlighting them) all appearances of that SIN *in that column*. Write the total in the bottom row marked "Self-nomin." Repeat that procedure for all other students in the Data Sheet. In Figure 3, we have highlighted the self-nominations by circling them.

f. *Quizzing your knowledge.* If you have read carefully the explanations above, you should now understand the meaning of all the numbers in a Data Sheet. Just to be sure, here are a few questions based on the data in Figure 3. Check your answers at the end of this chapter; if all of them are correct, you are ready for the next step.

1. What are the choices of student 1 for item 3?   _____
2. What are the choices of student 3 for item 7?   _____
3. Which student was absent or had his copy deleted?   _____
4. If you follow the transfer sequence, which is the
   first item left totally blank?   _____
5. Which student got the largest number of first choices for item 5?   _____
6. Which student evaluated his/her abilities most positively?   _____

C - Computing the Talent Scores

Forget for the time being the meaning of the talent scores; it will be explained in detail in the next chapter. Just focus on the mechanical operations needed to create these scores and place them correctly in the Score Sheet. Keep in mind that the basic role of **Tracking Talents** is to identify *only* those students who are judged by their peers to have the highest abilities in a variety of domains, at most the top 10% to 15%, which means the top three or four students in a group of 30. Because the other students will not be selected for special enrichment services, there is no need to compute their talent scores.

1. Basic scoring procedure

Your starting point will be the completed Data Sheet, and your endpoint will be a completed—but only partially filled—Score Sheet (see Figure 7). That document will contain the results for your group, including the peer scores, the teacher choices, and some of the self-nominations. Figure 4 shows an incomplete Score Sheet, based on the data in Figure 3. In the Score Sheet, each *row*, numbered from 1 to 30, represents a student. *All* students in a class list may *receive* peer nominations, even those who were absent when **Tracking Talents** was administered. If your class list has more than 30 names, you will need two copies of the Score Sheet. [*Suggestion*: staple immediately a copy of the class list to the Score Sheet; you will need it to identify the high scoring students.]

The *columns* represent the various items; their clustering reproduces the groupings in Table 1, not their sequence in the questionnaire. There is a different Score Sheet for each form; Figure 4 on page 22 shows a Form A Score Sheet. A column at the left of the items is reserved for gender identification; find each student's gender in the class list or on the cover page of the form and *circle* the appropriate letter in that column. We will explain in the next pages the meaning of the other elements in the Score Sheet.

The basic procedure follows the scoring principle described earlier (part B above), namely weighing choices according to their rank. It is a very simple four-step operation:
1. count all the *first* choices of a student and multiply by 3 (the number of points);
2. count all the *second* choices of that same student and multiply by 2 points;
3. count all the *third* choices; and
4. add the three partial totals to obtain a SUM called the *raw* talent score.

Figure 4
Partially Completed Score Sheet From Figure 3 Data

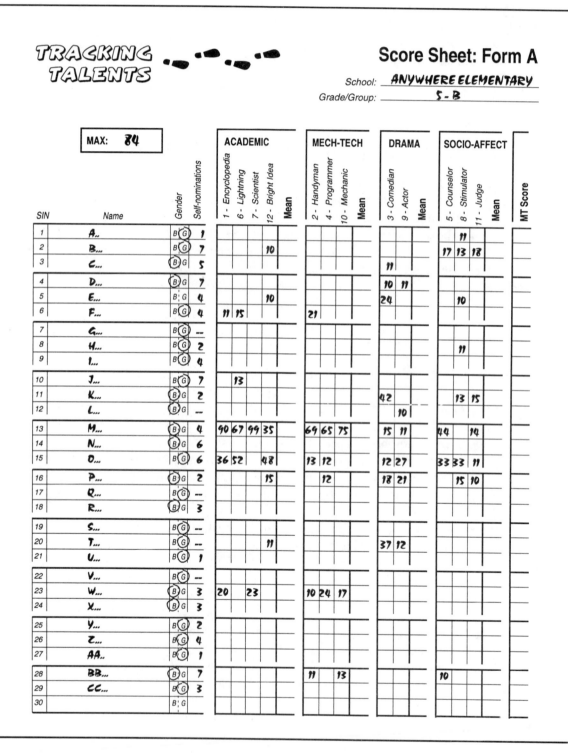

In other words, a *raw* talent score is basically the *sum of all the nominations received for a given item, each weighed according to its rank.*

Raw score (SUM) = (n. first choices x 3) + (n. second choices x 2) + n. third choices.
Unfortunately, that basic procedure has one major drawback that needs to be corrected.

2. Refining the basic procedure: Why and how

a. *Why we need to adjust the scores.* The basic procedure described above is highly influenced by the size of the group. Because we add points, students in large groups can obtain much bigger SUMs than those in small ones. For instance, in a group of 15 students, the maximum score a student could get would be 45, that is the SUM of all the first choices (3 x 15 = 45), including his or her first rank self-nomination. That maximum score would be twice as large in a group of 30 students (3 x 30 = 90). That bias due to group size would affect all other scores: For instance, getting half of the third choices translates into a SUM of 8 in a group of 16 students, and a SUM of 15 in a group of 30 students. The bottom line is that students in large groups would "appear" more talented, when in fact they would just be advantaged—unfairly—by the larger number of judges.

   Those who administer **Tracking Talents** to just one group and never compare results between groups can use the SUMs since the ranking of the students for each item *within their group* remains exactly the same whether or not we adjust the scores. But, most school districts who use **Tracking Talents** need to compare multiple groups (e.g., all fourth-graders, all students from Pine Tree Elementary), in which case the group size bias is a big hindrance. To facilitate these comparisons, a common scale becomes essential.

b. *Creating a new common scale.* We had to find a new scale that would be identical for all groups, whatever their size. The scale we chose is a *percentage scale*, in which 0% means that the student received no nominations for a given item, whereas 100% means that the student obtained a "perfect" score. What is a perfect score? Students get one when they receive *all* the first choices of their peers, and give themselves a first rank self-nomination. We will call that score the maximum (MAX) score. *All the talent scores will correspond to some percentage of that MAX score.* The MAX score changes from group to group depending on the number of respondents in the Data Sheet. For instance, with 25 valid copies in a group, the maximum will be 75 (3 x 25); for 21 valid copies, it will become 63, and so forth.

c. *How to make the adjustment.* First, you need to compute the MAX score for each group. To do so, just count the number of respondents in the Data Sheet and multiply by 3, which is the number of points given to first choices [*MAX = n. respondents x 3*]. *Do not* include the teacher. What is the maximum score for the group in Figure 3? It is 84 (28 x 3) since there are 28 respondents in that group (even though the highest SIN is 29, recall that student 12 is missing). Write the maximum score for your group in the space provided (MAX =) at the top of the Score Sheet (see Figure 4).

   The adjustment procedure is very simple: (1) divide *each* SUM (raw talent score) by that group's MAX score; (2) switch the decimal point two digits to the right (multiply by 100) to get percentages; and (3) round off to the nearest whole number. [*Note*: Rounding off means that if the *first* decimal is 5 or more, you add one unit. For instance, 15.4 remains 15, but 15.5 becomes 16.]

d. *Interpreting the adjusted item scores.* When they are divided by MAX (and multiplied by 100), all the talent scores become *percentages of the maximum score.* Students who obtain the maximum score in their group will get a talent score of 100, *whatever the size of their group.* Any student who gets all the second choices, including a second rank self-nomination, will obtain a talent score of 67 (two-thirds of the maximum). In the case of a "full house" of third choices, the talent score will be 33 (one-third of the maximum). Finally, all those who receive no nominations will have zero scores. In other words, any score (e.g., 8, 17, 23, 47, 71) will have the same meaning in every group; it will represent a percentage—always the same for a given score—of the best possible score (MAX) that a student could obtain *in that group.*

This percentage scale is very practical, not only because it makes between-group comparisons possible, but also because it uses a statistical index that is easy to interpret. Still, there is a small drawback: The corrected scores do advantage a little bit students in smaller groups because it is easier for 15 youngsters than for 30 to agree on their first—or second, or third—choice.

3. Computing item scores

We are now ready to create the Score Sheet. To illustrate the procedure, we will use the data in Figure 3 (Data Sheet), Figure 4 (incomplete Score Sheet), and Figure 7 (complete Score Sheet).

a. *Computing the first talent score.* Look at the item 1 data (Encyclopedia) in Figure 3: who got most of the first choices? It is student 13 with 24 of them. Since first choices are worth 3 points, we multiply 24 x 3, which gives a total of 72. Student 13 also received two second choices including his own self-nomination (had you noticed it?), each worth 2 points (2 x 2 = 4), but no third choices; his SUM for item 1 is 76 (72 + 4). We now divide that total by 84 (the MAX score for that group) and multiply by 100 to get a talent score of 90.

Suggestion: As you tally the frequencies of a student, it might help to cross them out so that those not yet counted will stand out. Moreover, to facilitate these computations, we have devised a special *Scoring Pad* (see Appendix D). Figure 5 shows how it is used to compute the three highest scores for item 1. As you become more familiar with the computations, you will rapidly discover that most SUMs can be computed *mentally,* except maybe for the two largest scores.

The score of 90 obtained by student 13 means that he got 90% of a perfect score for that item, not a bad result! That score appears in Figure 4 at the intersection of row 13 (his SIN) and the item 1 column. By the way, did you notice in Figure 3 that two students (7 and 19) did not choose student 13 at all? That is a bit strange in view of the quasi-perfect agreement of most other students on his first rank; but, it is a common phenomenon. Note that this student was also his teacher's first choice.

Figure 5
Example of Scoring Pad Use

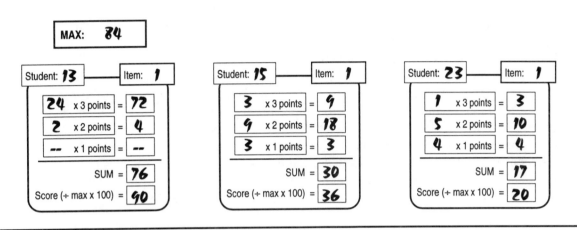

Let us go back to the Data Sheet. Who else got many nominations? SINs 15 and 23 each appear many times. In the case of student 15, Figures 3 and 5 show that she received three first choices, nine second choices, and three third choices; corrected by MAX, her SUM of 30 (9 + 18 + 3) becomes a talent score of 36. That number appears at the intersection of row 15 and the item 1 column in Figure 4. If we add the nominations of student 23 in Figure 3, he gets a score of 20 (see Figures 4 and 5).

b. *When to stop.* We recommend that you stop computing scores *when the SUM (number of points) drops below 7,* which corresponds to just a few nominations. In most groups (20–25 students), 7 points will give a talent score of 9 or 10. To make that decision, *do not* include in your count the self-nominations of these borderline cases, even more so if it is a first-rank choice; there are such cases in Figure 3. Look, for instance, at item 8 where student 4 has a SUM of 7, but 3 of these points come from a first-rank self-nomination, and he receives just two other (second-rank) peer choices. If we exclude the self-nomination (3 points), the SUM is just 4 points (2 x 2).

If you look at the item 1 data in Figure 3, are there any students left who would get at least 7 points? Yes, there is student 6 with two second-rank nominations and five third-rank ones, for a SUM of 9 points and a talent score of 11 (9 / 84 x 100). All other students (1, 2, 5, 7, 10, etc.) have just one or two nominations each; none of them would get more than 5 points. So, we stop right there, having computed only four talent scores for that first item. These four scores appear in the item 1 column (Encyclopedia) in Figure 4.

c. *Completing the item score computations.* Now, we go down to the next three rows in Figure 3, those for item 2, and look for the most popular SIN. Surprise! It's student 13 again with 17 first choices, 3 second choices, and 1 third choice, for a SUM of 58, which becomes a talent score of 69. The second most popular SIN is 6 with five first choices and three third choices; her talent score becomes (5 x 3) + 0 + (3 x 1) = 18 / 84 x 100 = 21. Three other students (15, 23, and 28) received enough nominations to compute a talent score (see Figure 4).

If we continued applying this procedure to the next 10 items, we would end up with Figure 4. Examine that figure closely; you will notice that only 16 different students (57% of the group) obtain at least one score of 10 or more (10+); five of them (students 1, 3, 8, 10, and 12) have just one such score, and many others have just two or three of them. In fact, students 13 and 15 get the lion's share, with no less than 36% (21/58) of all the 10+ scores. They could be said to possess multiple talents, at least in the eyes of their peers.

This is typical of the nomination technique: because we ask the judges to focus only on the best performers, we get only the best! (You could call them the "capital" SINs!) The rest of the choices are just "crumbs" spread all over the Score Sheet. To show you what the Score Sheet would look like if we had computed *all the possible scores*, we created an "all dressed" Figure 6; the empty cells (--) in that figure correspond to zero scores. Notice the large quantity of these zero scores among item scores, no less than 36% of the total (124/348); and there are more of them, proportionally, in the academic subgroup. This phenomenon will be explained in chapter 4. Another 40% or so (139/348) vary between one and five, showing how common it is for students to receive just one or two nominations, often a self-nomination or that of a best friend. In Figure 6, these low scores are distributed almost equally between all items and subgroups.

4. Computing subgroup and total scores

Here comes the last part of the peer score calculations: computing MEAN scores for the thematic subgroups, as well as an overall "multitalent" (MT) score. Again, you will need to "commute" back and forth between your Data Sheet and your Score Sheet.

a. *Computing subgroup scores.* To compute a subgroup score, you simply (a) add the item scores, (b) divide by the number of items in that subgroup, and (c) round off to the nearest integer. For instance, the Academic subgroup score of student 13 is computed as follows: $90 + 67 + 99 + 35 = 291$, and $291/4 = 73$. The result is the *mean* of the four item scores. When should you compute subgroup scores? Our recommendation: *only for the subgroups with at least one 15+ score or two 10+ scores*; in all other cases, the average would be too low to have any significance. Look at Figure 4: according to the above rule, for which students would you compute an Academic subgroup score? There are five students: 6, 13, 15, 16 (barely), and 23. In the Drama subgroup, you would compute scores for students 4, 5, 11, 13, 15, 16, and 20; and so forth.

To compute a subgroup score, you need item scores for *all* the items in that subgroup; in other words, you need to fill all the empty cells of that subgroup with the appropriate item scores; as described above, many of them will be zero scores. For example, look at student 6 in Figure 4; she already has scores of 11 and 15 in the Academic subgroup, but we need her scores for items 7 and 12 to compute an average for that subgroup. Similarly, she has a score of 21 for item 2 in the Mech/tech subgroup, which meets our criterion to compute a subgroup score; to do so, we need her scores for items 4 and 10 in that subgroup. These item scores will be computed as described above from the information in the Data Sheet.

On the other hand, student 1 has *only one* 10+ score in the Socioaffective subgroup, which is not enough to compute a subgroup score. If you scan Figure 4, you will see that some subgroup scores can be computed directly (e.g., students 2, 4, 13, etc.); but, in many more cases, some missing item scores need to be computed (e.g., students 5, 6, 11, 13,

Figure 6
Completely Filled Out Score Sheet From Figure 3 Data

TRACKING TALENTS

Score Sheet: Form A

School: __ANYWHERE ELEMENTARY__
Grade/Group: __5-B__

MAX: **84**

SIN	Name	Gender	Self-nominations	ACADEMIC 1-Encyclopedia	6-Lightning	7-Scientist	12-Bright Idea	Mean	MECH-TECH 2-Handyman	4-Programmer	10-Mechanic	Mean	DRAMA 3-Comedian	9-Actor	Mean	SOCIO-AFFECT 5-Counselor	8-Stimulator	11-Judge	Mean	MT Score
1	A...	G	1	1	2	--	--	1	5	--	2	2	6	1	4	--	11	6	6	3
2	B...	G	7	5	4	2	10	5	1	2	2	2	--	5	3	17	13	18	16	7
3	C...	B	5	--	--	1	--	--	2	6	5	4	11	7	9	2	2	2	2	4
4	D...	B	7	--	1	1	6	2	2	2	--	1	10	11	11	2	8	4	5	5
5	E...	B	4	1	--	2	10	3	4	--	2	2	24	7	16	1	10	6	6	7
6	F...	G	4	11	15	5	6	9	21	4	--	8	--	4	2	8	4	2	5	6
7	G...	G	--	2	2	1	--	1	--	1	2	1	--	4	2	--	2	7	3	2
8	H...	G	2	--	--	1	--	--	2	--	--	1	1	4	3	5	11	1	6	3
9	I...	G	4	--	--	2	--	1	2	4	--	2	4	--	2	--	8	4	4	2
10	J...	G	7	5	13	1	5	6	5	5	--	3	--	6	3	5	2	6	4	4
11	K...	B	2	--	--	--	7	2	2	--	2	1	42	--	21	--	13	15	9	8
12	L...	B	--	--	1	--	--	--	--	--	--	--	2	10	6	--	--	--	--	2
13	M...	B	4	90	67	99	35	73	69	65	75	70	15	11	13	44	5	14	21	44
14	N...	B	6	--	--	2	--	1	5	1	6	4	--	--	--	6	2	2	3	2
15	O...	B	6	36	52	8	48	36	13	12	1	9	12	27	20	33	33	11	26	23
16	P...	B	2	7	7	2	15	8	2	12	7	7	18	21	20	7	15	10	11	12
17	Q...	G	--	2	1	--	--	1	--	--	--	--	--	1	1	--	6	2	3	1
18	R...	B	3	4	4	1	4	3	5	2	1	3	--	1	1	--	--	4	1	2
19	S...	G	--	2	4	--	4	3	--	--	--	--	2	4	3	4	--	4	3	2
20	T...	G	--	--	--	--	11	3	--	5	--	2	37	12	25	4	6	4	5	9
21	U...	G	1	--	--	--	--	--	--	4	--	1	--	--	--	--	--	--	--	
22	V...	G	--	--	--	--	--	--	--	--	--	--	--	4	2	5	--	2	2	1
23	W...	B	3	20	5	23	--	12	10	24	17	17	--	4	2	--	--	--	--	8
24	X...	B	3	--	--	--	1	--	--	2	4	2	--	1	1	--	7	4	4	2
25	Y...	G	2	2	--	--	--	1	--	--	--	--	2	5	4	--	1	7	3	2
26	Z...	G	4	--	4	--	4	2	1	1	--	1	4	2	3	4	7	--	4	3
27	AA..	G	1	1	--	--	--	--	4	1	--	2	--	--	--	4	--	1	2	1
28	BB...	B	7	--	4	1	8	3	11	5	13	10	2	8	5	10	2	4	5	6
29	CC...	G	3	--	1	2	--	1	1	6	4	4	4	2	3	5	--	4	3	3
30		B/G																		

etc.). Try calculating some of them, then check your results in Figure 7; all the subgroup scores that should be computed according to our rules and the data in Figure 4 appear in Figure 7. In terms of peer scores, Figure 7 is the complete Score Sheet that results from the Figure 3 Data Sheet. Compare Figures 6 and 7 to see how "naked" a *complete* Score Sheet looks from the *all dressed* one. The comparison shows the uselessness of most scores, about 75% of them, because of their low value (5 or less).

b. *Subgroup score distributions.* Do not expect the subgroup scores to vary as much as the item scores, since the abilities measured in each subgroup are not that closely related to expect equally high or low scores for each student. This is easy to see in Figure 7. For instance, student 11 has the highest score (42) for item 3 (Comedian), but a zero score for item 9 (Actor) in the same subgroup. You will observe that the highest subgroup scores are rarely as high as the highest item scores. As shown in the all dressed Figure 6, there are also fewer zero scores at the subgroup level because the chances of getting a few nominations here and there are higher over three or four items than for a single item.

c. *Computing a total (MT) score.* As we will explain in chapter 4, the total score, labeled MT for *multitalent*, is the *least* useful of all the **Tracking Talents** scores. But, if you decide that you need that information, just proceed as for subgroup scores; first compute any missing subgroup scores, then add them and divide by 4. We have included in Figure 7 three MT scores; for two of them we had the four subgroup scores, but for the other (student 16) we had to compute a Mech/tech score (see Figure 4). Note that the MT scores vary even less than subgroup scores; our multitalented student 13 obtained a total score of only 44, compared to subgroup mean scores of 73 and 70; the next highest total score (23) is almost twice as small.

Suggestion: You will probably find it easier to analyze your Score Sheet if you highlight the highest (2, 3, or 4) item and subgroup scores.

d. *Re-quizzing your knowledge.* Now, the contents of Figure 7 should be totally clear to you. Just to make sure, let's see how well you can answer the following questions. Check you answers at the end of this chapter; if all of them are correct, you are ready for the next step.

---

1. Which student is the best Programmer?   _____
2. Which students are judged to be the two most creative?   _____
3. What is the score of student 20 for item 3?   _____
4. What score did the best Comedian get for item 9?   _____
5. How many first choices did the second best Counselor receive for that item?   _____

D - Transferring the Teacher and Self-nominations

To complete your Score Sheet, you need to transfer from the Data Sheet the teacher and self-nominations. Our recommended procedure is described on the page 30.

Figure 7
Completed Score Sheet From Figure 3 Data

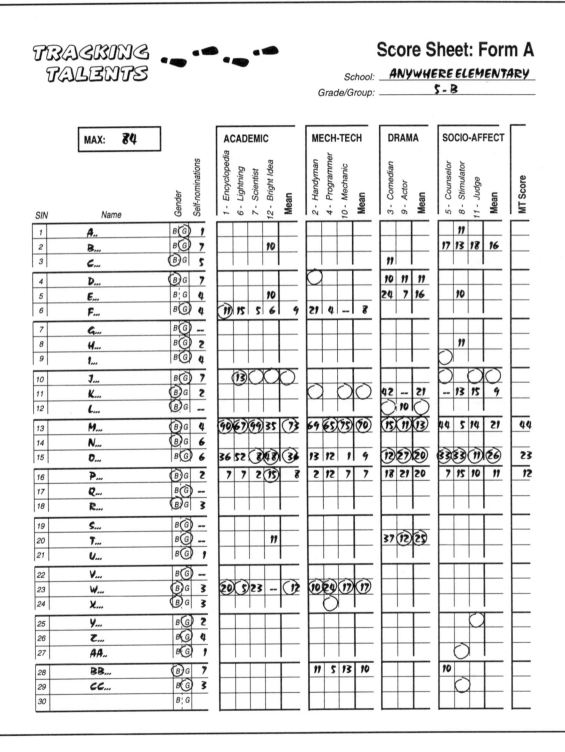

a. *Transferring the teacher nominations.* The best way we have found to transfer the teacher choices to the Score Sheet is to circle *all* the appropriate cells, even empty ones. For example, the teacher's three choices for item 1 (Encyclopedia) are, in order, students 13, 23, and 6. Look at Figure 7, and you will see these students' scores circled in the item 1 column. Notice that the peers' second choice (SIN 15) was not named by the teacher. Notice also that the teacher's three choices (23, 4, and 11) for item 2 (Handyman) differ completely from the peers' three highest scores (students 13, 6, and 15). A few subgroup scores in Figure 7 have been circled; yet, teachers are not asked for subgroup nominations. The circles mean that these students received teacher nominations—any rank—for at least half of the items in that subgroup.

b. *Transferring the self-nominations.* Self-nominations pose a special problem that we will discuss in detail in part C of chapter 4. For the time being, just transfer the *number* of self-nominations from the bottom of the Data Sheet to the proper column in the Score Sheet.

E - Checklist of Scoring Operations

A. *Preparations*
1. Discard any student copy with fewer than 12 nominations.
2. Order all valid copies according to the respondents' SIN, with student 1 on top.
3. Place doubtful copies underneath (also ordered), and the teacher's copy (if any) at the bottom of the pile.
4. If there are more than 30 respondents (Data Sheet), or 30 students in the group (Score Sheet), have ready two copies of the relevant form.

B. *Completing the Data Sheet*
1. Transfer respondents' SINs and answers down each column, beginning at left with student 1, and skipping rows when you encounter missing data. Check for duplicate numbers in each trio. Delete the lowest ranked duplicate.
2. [If relevant] Check if the data in each doubtful copy partially resemble the more popular choices in the Data Sheet. If so, include that copy. If not, discard it.
3. Add the teacher's nominations in the rightmost column.
4. Circle (or highlight) the self-nominations of each student. Enter the *total* in the bottom row.

C. *Completing the Score Sheet*
1. Enter the genders in column B-G.
2. Compute and enter the MAX score.
3. Compute item scores for all the students who get at least 7 points (excluding self-nominations) from any combination of 1st, 2nd, or 3rd choices. Use the formula below.
   Score = SUM / MAX x 100, where SUM = (1st choices x 3) + (2nd choices x 2) + 3rd choices.
4. Compute subgroup scores for all students who have at least one 15+ score or two 10+ scores in a given subgroup. First, compute any missing item scores, then average them.

5. If you want some total scores, do operation 4 above for all subgroups of the target students, then compute the average of the subgroup scores.
6. Highlight the highest (2-3-4) item and subgroup scores.
7. Transfer the teacher's nominations by circling all the relevant cells, even empty ones.
8. Circle the subgroup scores of the students who received teacher nominations for most items in that subgroup.
9. Transfer the number of self-nominations from the Data Sheet to the proper column.

Answers to quiz on page 21 (about the Data Sheet)

1. The item 3 choices of student 1 are 16, 11, and 5.
2. The item 7 choices of student 3 are 13, blank, and blank.
3. The deleted student is 12.
4. The first completely blank item is item 11 of student 8.
5. Student 13 got the most first choices (n = 11) for item 5.
6. Four students (2, 4, 10, and 28) had the largest number of self-nominations, namely seven.

Answers to quiz on page 28 (about the Score Sheet)

1. The best Programmer is student 13.
2. Students 15 and 13 have the two highest creativity scores (item 12: Bright Idea) respectively.
3. Student 20's score for item 3 is 37.
4. The best Comedian (item 3) is student 11, with a talent score of 42. His score for item 9 (Actor) is zero (see Figure 7).
5. The second best Counselor is SIN 15 who received 6 first choices for item 5 (see Figure 3).

Chapter Four

❋ ❋

Interpreting Tracking Talents

Since their creation a decade ago, the **Tracking Talents** PTSNFs have been used mostly for research purposes. Because just a few teachers and program coordinators have administered them to select students for enrichment services, there is yet little accumulated knowledge and practical experience on their proper use and interpretation. The contents of this chapter remain tentative, and will be expanded as these forms become more and more popular, and as we get feedback from users on the particular problems they encounter and the solutions they devise. Thus, the following text is offered more as a set of general guidelines than well-tested practices.

Two cautionary notes

First, because **Tracking Talents** is a psychometric instrument, its administration and interpretation should be supervised by a professional who possesses enough knowledge about testing issues to understand the technical questions discussed in this chapter and the next one. Even if **Tracking Talents** was carefully written and tested, just like any other good psychological test it has limits: limits imposed by its specific content, by biases inherent in human judgments, by statistical imprecisions, and so forth. Thus, care must be exercised in weighing the information provided by these forms.

Second, there is yet very limited *concurrent validity* information (see chapter 5, part D.6) concerning most of the abilities assessed in both forms of **Tracking Talents**. In other words, except for academic talents, which we were able to compare to school grades, we do not know to what extent the peer, self, or teacher judgments represent "real" differences in performance. For that reason, caution should be exercised when interpreting the Score Sheet data.

This chapter covers four major subjects: (a) an important discussion of the relationship between peer judgments and the distribution of talent scores; (b) the interpretation of peer talent scores and teacher judgments; (c) the special problems limiting the use of the self-nominations; and (d) final comments and suggestions.

A - Peer Agreement versus Score Distributions

The scores derived from peer judgments have a very special characteristic: their distribution differs totally from the well-known "normal" or bell-shaped curve. Moreover, that special distribution is directly influenced by the perceptiveness of the judges, namely how well they agree when assessing the abilities of their peers. A correct interpretation of the peer talent scores requires a minimum knowledge of their very atypical distribution. Let us examine that question more closely.

a. *A special type of reliability.* The first and most important quality that all peer nomination forms must possess is a high degree of agreement between the peer "judges" on their choice of the best (second best, third best) for each ability measured. Without such agreement, called inter-peer agreement (IPA), the task would be totally worthless, since one would not know whom to believe when different judges give different choices. Inter-peer agreement is one form of reliability; in fact, the most important form of reliability for judgments of psychological traits (abilities, personality, etc.). The level of IPA directly affects the shape of the distribution of talent scores. To better grasp that impact, let us look at various hypothetical situations.

b. *The case of total disagreement.* Imagine, at one extreme, that the students totally disagree among themselves, that the nominations made by any one judge have nothing in common with those of any other judge. In other words, there is total anarchy, everyone picking SIN numbers at random in the class list. In that worse case—and very improbable—scenario, no student would receive more nominations than any other, except for small differences due to random effects. The practical impact of such a situation is that the typical student would receive one choice of each rank *on average*, which would give him or her a raw score (SUM) of 6 (3 + 2 + 1) or something close to that. The corresponding talent score would be 7 in a group of 30 (6/90 x 100), 8 in a group of 25 (6/75 x 100), and 10 in a group of 20 (6/60 x 100). Almost all the students in such a group would obtain for every item a talent score close to that typical random score of 7 to 10. Moreover, the distribution of the scores would have a mean of about 7 to 10, with a very small standard deviation, most of the scores being bunched around that low mean. The range would probably not exceed 15 or 20 points, more or less. Indeed, that is the only case where the score distribution would look like a normal distribution. That situation of total unreliability is shown in Figure 8, graph A.

c. *The case of perfect agreement.* Imagine, on the other hand, that our student judges agree perfectly among themselves. Then, one student would receive *all* the first choices of these judges (including a first choice self-nomination); this would give him or her the MAX score, equivalent to a talent score of 100. A second student would receive all the second choices (worth 2 points) from these same judges who are in perfect agreement, plus a second-rank self-nomination; this would give him or her a talent score of 67, two thirds of the

Figure 8
Different Levels of Inter-Peer Agreement

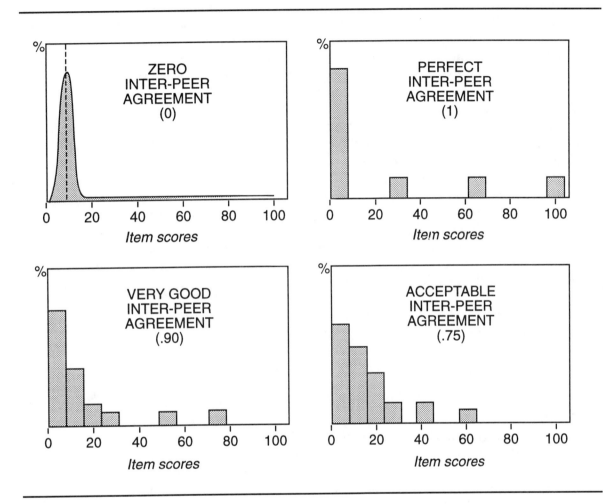

maximum. Finally, a third student would get all the third choices (1 point) and thus obtain a talent score of 33 for that ability. At that point, there would be no nominations left to distribute. Consequently, all the other students in the group would get a score of *zero*. In that utopian psychometric situation, the distribution of the talent scores in any such group of perfectly agreeing judges would be highly asymmetrical, with one 100, one 67, one 33, and a large number of zero scores, just like the distribution shown in Figure 8.

That bizarre distribution is the result of perfect agreement among judges. You can see now why talkative students, those who say out loud their choices during the test administration, can influence some of their peers, and artificially increase the consensus among judges, thus giving the erroneous impression of inter-peer agreement. A high IPA level must not be the result of social influence phenomena. It must be attained because the judges are good perceivers and because what they are asked to evaluate is clearly described and easily observable.

d. *Usual distributions.* The above situation of perfect agreement almost never happens, even among adult judges. Those who emerge with high scores within the group have little chance of receiving either all the first, second, or third choices. What we find more commonly is a series of scores larger than zero, with just one high score (> 50), but still far from the maximum, two or three moderate ones (> 20), and a similar number of modest (10+) scores. Just go back to Figure 6 and examine any column of item scores; you will realize how accurate that statement is. Look also at the tentative normative data—based on the small Phase III sample—presented in Appendix C for the item, subgroup, and MT scores in Forms A and B; they consist of percentages of students for various score categories.

This relationship between peer agreement and score distribution is fascinating: it shows that the nominating process contains its own safety valve. Here is how it works. If, for a particular item, a group of students cannot identify easily the top two or three best among them, they will spread their choices among a larger number of "likely" candidates. Consequently, instead of one or two high scores, we will observe a larger number of more moderate scores (≤ 30) and conclude that the group contains no outstanding student for that particular ability domain. In other words, even though a really outstanding student might go undetected within a group of unreliable judges, at least there is little risk that they will wrongly identify as talented individuals who are barely above average.

The level of IPA can be statistically measured. The formula is mathematically equivalent to what is known as Cronbach's alpha, a coefficient of homogeneity for a group of items. IPA coefficients look just like correlation coefficients: they vary between 0 (no agreement whatsoever) and 1.00 (perfect agreeement). Values of .80 or more are considered quite satisfactory (Anastasi & Urbina, 1997). Values between .70 and .80 are judged borderline, and those below .70 are questionable.

Graph C in Figure 8 shows the typical profile of a very good item with an IPA coefficient of around .90, whereas graph D in that same figure illustrates the typical look of an item with an IPA coefficient of .75. The first four columns of Table 3 in chapter 5 (part C.2) contain average IPA coefficients for all the items in the two final forms of **Tracking Talents**. It is remarkable that the values do not change much from one column to the next because the degree of agreement depends significantly on the type of ability assessed. So, whatever the sample—as long as it is large enough—the level of agreement will be highly predictable from the item content. For instance, the IPA values are much larger for items like Encyclopedia, Comedian, Hercules, or Artist, whereas students have much more difficulty agreeing about abilities like Counselor, Stimulator, or Judge. Compare these IPA values with the data in Appendix C; you will notice that more reliable items have larger percentages of zero scores as well as high scores.

e. *Checking for "bad" groups.* Bad groups are those in which the IPA coefficient is very low for many of the items, much lower than in most groups. How can you determine if a particular group of students has chronically low IPA levels? Just count the number of 40+ scores across the 12 items; if there are fewer than four or five (the average is nine), then the level of peer agreement within that group is questionable. Figure 4 contains 10, most of them received by students 13 and 15; it shows very good agreement within that particular group. [In a situation of perfect agreement, there would be 24 of them, 12 score of 100 and 12 scores of 67.]

There can be many reasons for such low group agreement: a lack of carefulness when completing **Tracking Talents**, insufficient interactions between students to increase shared knowledge about abilities, the presence of cliques or gangs with some implicit peer pressure to restrict one's choices to gang members, strong gender separations leading each group to select within one's own gender, and so forth. If you observe few high scores within in a particular group, you should examine the possibility of readministering **Tracking Talents** to that group after checking with the teacher about possible explanations for that phenomenon.

f. *Summary.* Not only is there a direct relationship between IPA reliability and score distributions, but there is also a close relationship between IPA values and the number of high scores: the more student judges agree among themselves, the more chances there are that one student will obtain a talent score of 80 or more, just like the quasi-perfect score of student 13 for item 7 (Scientist) in Figure 7. And, as explained above, that is an excellent "security blanket" against using unreliable information. IPA unreliability *automatically* produces low talent scores, thus reducing the chances of selecting the wrong students for an enrichment program.

B - Interpreting Peer and Teacher Nominations

This second part will focus on peer nominations, using the teacher choices as cross-validating information. We will examine successively the item scores, the subgroup scores, and the total score.

1. Interpreting the item scores

When the first experimental forms of **Tracking Talents** were created, we were hoping that the *item* peer scores would be reliable enough to be used for screening purposes. As shown in the preceding section, our results indicate that, for most of them, the reliability indices (IPA) are quite satisfactory. Moreover, as explained above, low reliabilities are associated with the absence of very high scores, thus with fewer chances of students being selected in such cases. So, we do not hesitate to recommend using item scores as the *predominant* level of analysis. Here are some comments and advice on the use of these item scores in the selection procedure.

a. *Pairing items with program goals.* The following advice will probably appear self-evident: use only those items that are logically related to the goals and content of the enrichment service. For instance, there is no reason to look at art scores if the service offers enrichment in mathematics. On the other hand, if **Tracking Talents** items became the source of ideas to create enrichment services specifically targeted at them, we would consider that achievement as something to be very proud of. For instance, there is a glaring dearth of enrichment services for students (mostly boys) who show outstanding mechanical or technical abilities; yet, peers and teachers have little difficulty identifying students who appear quite talented in these related fields.

b. *The meaning of high scores.* What are high talent scores? There is no simple answer to that question. Talent scores tend to vary in size depending on a certain number of factors; apart from individual differences in ability, the major ones are peer agreement linked with item content. For instance, because peer agreement is so much better for academic or physical abilities, we regularly observe for these abilities higher scores than for social ones; in social areas, the judges—peers and teachers alike—have much more difficulty agreeing on those who are best. This means that the selection criterion cannot be the same for all abilities. For instance, a criterion score of 40 will select on average the top 5% (1 or 2 per group on average) in terms of academic talent, but less than 2% of the students if the target abilities are Counselor, Judge, or Sociable (see Appendix C).

Should a talent score be judged high only if at least half of the students name a particular student, irrespective of the rank of that nomination? Half of the first choices will produce a talent score of 50, but half of the third choices will create a score of only 17. Still, half of the third choices is not a bad result in a nomination process. Moreover, keep in mind that a given talent score may result from different combinations of first-, second-, and third-rank choices. For instance, a score of 20 could represent either 20% of all first choices, 40% of all second choices, or 60% of all third choices, as well as hundreds of other combinations of these three ranks. Because scores of 20 or more represent on average not more than 18% of all scores for a typical item, that threshold could be used as the lower limit of "moderate" talent scores, with scores of 40 or more being definitely high scores, if only because their incidence does not exceed 5% on average.

c. *About hair-splitting.* Whether nominations are made by peers, by teachers, or even by the subjects themselves, the process is inherently imprecise: just delete one first choice and the talent score will drop by 3 or 4 points. So, beware of splitting hairs! You will frequently encounter tied scores or scores that do not differ by more than 3 or 4 points, especially in the bottom half of the scale: *consider as tied any two scores that differ by less than 5 points.*

d. *Within-group versus district-level selection criteria.* Spontaneously, program coordinators might be tempted to choose a predetermined number (or percentage) of students *from each group,* for example the two or three top scorers. That might not be the best selection strategy; it assumes that abilities are distributed fairly and equally among all groups of students, with each class having the same number of "best" students in any area. As other assessments have shown time and again, fair distributions are the exception rather than the norm. We believe that it is preferable to establish a school-level or district-level criterion, rank all the best students according to their talent scores, and select those with the highest scores, even if this means more students selected from some groups or schools than from others.

Some will immediately notice that even this solution is not ideal. Indeed, it is possible that some students could get a lower score in their own group just because it happens that there is one (or two) exceptional peer(s) in the same group receiving a large majority of the choices; these students might have fared better in another group. It is also possible for a talented student to belong to a "bad" group (see part A), in which low peer agreement reduces the chances of getting a high score. In other words, just like any other form of ability assessment, peer nominations are not a panacea!

e. *Comparing peer and teacher choices.* Cardinal (1992) examined in detail the relationship between peer and teacher nominations. A summary of her observations appears in chapter

5, part D.4. Cardinal's study showed that, by and large, peer and teacher judgments are moderately correlated, and that the degree of agreement between these two sources depends significantly on what particular ability is being assessed. For instance, there is a much closer relationship in the case of academic talents than social ones. Table 6 in chapter 5 presents the peer-teacher correlations for all items in Forms A and B. When compared with the IPA coefficients in Table 3, these values clearly show that items with high peer agreement also show high peer-teacher agreement. In other words, some abilities are much easier to observe and assess than others.

We mentioned at the beginning of this chapter that teacher choices could be used as cross-validating information for the peer scores. If the choices match, so much the better, and if they do not, then a decision has to be made about the relative validity of the two judgments. Just keep in mind that the peer scores represent the average of over 20 individual perceptions, whereas the teacher's choices "suffer" from the subjectivity of single judgments. So, do not automatically lean toward the teacher's choices, especially in the case of abilities that are not commonly practiced in the school environment.

If you completed your Score Sheet as recommended in chapter 3, you should see easily how frequently the highest peer scores are circled (teacher's choices), indicating peer-teacher agreement irrespective of rank. For their part, circled low peer scores will signal partial agreement, while circled empty cells will highlight clear disagreement between the two sources.

Figure 7 shows very interesting phenomena in this respect. Here are just a few comments. First, both the peers and the teacher agree generally that students 13 and 15 clearly distinguish themselves from all their peers because of their multiple talents. But, while the peers give student 13 almost twice as many choices (as shown by the MT scores), the teacher rates both about equally (see her *ranked* choices in Figure 3). Second, over one-third (13/36) of the teacher's choices correspond to empty cells in Figure 7. For instance, the teacher gave five of her choices to student 10, who remained almost totally ignored by her peers. There would be many more interesting observations to point out, but space …! Anyway, we hope that these comments will give you a glimpse of how rich the peer-teacher comparisons can be, especially if they are discussed with the teacher and—why not?—the students.

f. *Checking for gender bias*. Gender differences are quite normal, since abilities do not seem to be distributed equally between boys and girls. For instance, you will probably observe that boys tend to receive more high scores than girls on items in the physical or mechanical/technical subgroups, as well as on the item Comedian, whereas the opposite will probably happen with items in the arts or socioaffective subgroups (see chapter 5, part D.5, and Gagné, 1993c). While some critics might argue that this is a bias created by stereotypical perceptions of male and female gender roles, we do not think so, especially since similar disparities were observed with teacher nominations, most of them from female teachers in elementary and middle schools. In other words, these gender differences have nothing to do with the bias announced in the title.

The gender bias we want to point out here is the tendency for students of each sex to nominate members of their own sex disproportionately. As mentioned at the beginning of chapter 2, this can disadvantage the minority when the gender split is far from 50/50. For instance, suppose that your group of 24 students has a two-thirds proportion (16/24) of boys. In that case, you should check if girls receive their fair share of high scores, especially on items that are traditionally female-oriented. Table 6 in chapter 5 gives the distribution of genders for the 24 final items (based on data from Gagné, 1993c). Look also at the teacher nominations to see if there are systematic gender differences between the peer and teacher choices.

Unfortunately, there is no simple corrective procedure if you find that one gender is not being fairly treated in this peer nomination process. One possibility could be to fix a lower threshold for the "forgotten" gender, but it is difficult to tell how well this would work, especially if the scores of the biased-against gender were really low.

g. *Any risk of a "best friend" bias*? At the beginning of Project PAIRS, we were worried about a potential "best friend" bias, which is a tendency for students to name their best friend much more often than he or she deserves it. For that reason, we asked all students participating in the data collections to write their best friend's SIN on the cover page of the experimental forms of *Tracking Talents*; we then examined how often these best friends were nominated. These analyses, and many more, are summarized in part D.2 of chapter 5. In a nutshell, while there was a clear tendency for the students to name their best friend somewhat generously (but not as much as themselves!), these nominations mostly appeared on items belonging to the two social abilities subgroups. Moreover, just as we discovered with self-nominations, these "best friend" nominations did not affect the reliability of the talent scores. Consequently, users should not worry about such a bias.

2. Interpreting the subgroup scores

In theory, aggregating items and computing group scores should create more stable, thus reproducible measures than the item scores. In practice, many factors that are too complex to examine here do not guarantee that such will be the case. Here are a few comments concerning the use of subgroup talent scores.

a. *All groups are not born equal*. Both forms of *Tracking Talents* offer four subgroups, each composed of two to four items. Because the correlations between item scores vary considerably, there is no direct relationship between the number of items and the reliability of a subgroup score. For instance, based on the results of various factor analyses, the most homogeneous subgroups of items were found to be the academic, the physical, and the visual arts, whereas the socioaffective, social influence, and mech/tech subgroups showed more fragility.

Some expected subgroups did not even materialize. For instance, we were hoping that students would be able to differentiate between intellectual (e.g., Lightning, Encyclopedia) and creative (e.g., Bright idea, Original) abilities. But, both sets were judged to belong to the same type of ability; in other words, the students judged that the best in "intellectual" abilities also tended to be the most "creative." It was also difficult to separate items that we placed a priori in a group called "social-ethical skills," as compared to items we judged beforehand to measure "sociability" or "social influence." We finally decided to maintain the distinction, but it manifests itself only partially in our results (see chapter 5, part D.3). In summary, because of these imperfections, the subgroup scores should be interpreted with as much caution as the item scores.

b. *Special points to watch for.* The interpretation of the subgroup scores does not differ much from the item-level analyses. Here are a few more specific considerations to keep in mind.

1. Just as we pointed out in the case of item scores, choose subgroup scores that measure abilities that are directly related to those required by the enrichment service for which the students are being screened.

2. Even though the basic analysis of the distributions presented in part A of this chapter remains generally applicable to subgroup scores, their statistical characteristics differ somewhat from those of item scores. For instance, whereas one can expect on average 5% of 40+ item scores, such is not the case with subgroup scores. The variability of subgroup scores is much smaller because of the phenomenon of regression to the mean when measures are not perfectly correlated: the number of high scores is drastically reduced, as well as the number of zero scores. Moreover, all other things kept equal, that regression effect should have a more significant impact on the larger four-item subgroups than on the two-item ones. Users should keep in mind these differences, either (a) when comparing item scores with subgroup scores, or (b) when choosing threshold scores for selection purposes.

3. The gender differences mentioned in relation to item scores will inevitably reappear at the level of subgroup scores (e.g., a predominance of boys in the physical and mechanical fields). For instance, look at the gender of students with the highest scores in the mech/tech subgroup; but, note also that these tendencies are just that: tendencies. For example, the highest scores in the socioaffective subgroup (see Figure 7) belong to three boys (SINs 11, 13, 16) and two girls (2, 15).

    Gender differences manifest themselves in another way at the subgroup level, namely through differences in the strength of the subgroups when boys' and girls' scores are analyzed separately. For instance, the mechanical/technical subgroup comes out clearly when we factor analyze the boys' scores, but remains partly hidden when looking strictly at the girls' scores (see Gagné & Talbot, 1995; Leblanc, 1998). Practically speaking, it means that you should not expect equal percentages of boys and girls among the high scorers in any subgroup, except maybe in the case of academic talents. Again, if the gender distribution of a group is far from 50/50, let's say 65/35 or more, you should watch for possible underevaluation of the smaller group's abilities.

4. Finally, just like you did for item scores, use teacher nominations as cross-validating information for the peer scores, keeping in mind that the teachers are *not necessarily* the most valid source of information on students' abilities. Just look for major discrepancies and try to verify with the teachers the reasons for them. Teacher choices could be especially useful to check for the potential gender bias mentioned above.

3. Multitalent scores: to use or not to use?

As described in chapter 3, a global mean score can be computed for each form from the subgroup scores. We decided early on to label it "multitalent score" (MT) instead of total score, because the term *multitalent* conveys more clearly the nature of that combination of items from different subgroups. Adding related items to create subgroup scores makes sense because of the similarity in content; but, when we add subgroup scores we are, to some degree at least, adding apples and oranges. Moreover, the quasi-totality of enrichment services offered in North American school districts target populations of students with very specific talents or gifts (e.g., academic enrichment programs, music programs, elite sports programs, and so forth). Thus, because of its mixture of qualitatively distinct abilities, the MT score should be the least frequently used of all *Tracking Talents* scores in the context of talent identification.

But, there might be other reasons to identify MT individuals. For example, there is some literature on the special career choice problems of these persons who can succeed in almost any profession they decide to pursue (e.g., Delisle, 1985; Silverman, 1993); it is sometimes called "the overchoice syndrome" (Pask-McCartney & Salomone, 1988). It might be helpful to pinpoint these students early and organize a series of counseling activities focusing on career planning. Otherwise, these youngsters might have problems dealing with their time management as they try to develop multiple talents simultaneously; again, group counseling might help them share problems and coping strategies. Users will no doubt find many other valid reasons to get interested in that special target group. Because MT scores could be relevant to some screening purposes, here are some descriptive and cautionary comments about them.

a. *Psychometric relevance.* Since the first psychometric study of *Tracking Talents* in 1988, MT scores have been computed and their reliability checked through homogeneity and stability assessments (see chapter 5, parts C and D). These checks have shown repeatedly that MT scores have adequate reliability. The item and subgroup scores are sufficiently correlated to give psychometric relevance to these scores (see Table 5). In other words, there is an underlying tendency for most abilities to be slightly related, to entertain what specialists in ability testing call a *positive manifold*: the more talented in one ability reappear more often among the best in another ability, even in very distinct fields (e.g., arts and sports). This positive manifold emerges clearly in the correlation matrix of subgroup scores presented in Table 5 (see chapter 5, part D.3). It is these low (sometimes moderate) and recurring correlations between items and subgroups that justify the computation of MT scores. The higher these MT scores, the more they reflect the presence of multiple talents.

b. *A few notes about multitalent.* Multitalent is not as rare a phenomenon as most educators tend to believe. Within the framework of Project PAIRS, it was possible to examine closely the incidence of multitalented individuals. Using Phase I data (see chapter 5), we examined the item scores of over 2,400 students for whom we had peer nominations for 20 different abilities (Gagné, 1998b). We decided to label "talented" any student who was among the three best in his or her group for *any* of these 20 abilities. We created a special MT score that corresponded to the number of times that student appeared among the three best of his or her group; that score could vary from a minimum of 0 to a maximum of 20.

We found that, even with 20 distinct abilities assessed, 53% of the students in that large sample *never* appeared among the three best in their own group, as judged by their peers. On the other hand, 16% were judged by their peers to be among the three best on at least five different abilities, and 40% of them (6% of the total) emerged among the three best on *at least 10* of the 20 abilities measured. So, it seems that some individuals have a facility to excel in many areas, as demonstrated by students 13 and 15 in Figure 7, whereas a large percentage, almost half of that large sample, never stand out enough to be labeled talented. It is that phenomenon of multitalent that explains and justifies the computation of MT scores. But, we have yet to see enrichment services that target that specific population. This is why, as interesting as multitalented individuals may be, these scores should be used with caution as screening tools.

c. *Variability*. If you decide to use MT scores, remember that they vary much less than item scores, and less than even subgroup scores. In the Phase III study, Leblanc (1998) found only 0.8% 30+ MT scores. That can be seen in Figure 6; notice that the highest MT score, that of student 13, is just 44. In a way, this sum is far below the theoretical maximum of 100; yet, it means that this one student received almost 45% of all the points—mostly in the form of first and second choices—attributed by all the judges in that group across all 12 items. This is quite an achievement for that young boy. Indeed, only 11 students (1.5%) in the Phase III sample obtained a 40+ MT score (see Appendix C). Note also that the second highest MT score, the 23 obtained by student 15, is only about half as high, and falls below the 30+ threshold. We then go down to 12 points for the third place MT score. As you can see, the level falls sharply and rapidly.

C - Interpreting Self-Nominations

You may wonder why we have left self-nominations aside until almost the end of this chapter. It gives the impression that their value is more questionable than the information gathered from the two other sources. Well, that is just the case. Let us look more closely at some of the things we know about them before discussing the interpretation problem they pose.

Thanks to Massé (1992), we have a good deal of information about the way students use the "privilege" of choosing themselves as talented in any field assessed by ***Tracking Talents***. Section D.1 in chapter 5 summarizes most of her results. Keep in mind that all the results in chapter 5 are based on the experimental instruments, in which we requested four choices instead of the three used in the final forms; more choices slightly increase the incidence of self-nominations. We will use Leblanc's (1998) master's thesis, in which he reported the results of a validation study with the two final forms, to update some of the data about self-nominations.

a. *Incidence of self-nominations*. As described in chapter 5, students have a "generous" view of their abilities. In the experimental studies with the original forms, they named themselves no less than five times (out of 12 items) on average, which represents a rate of 40%. For his part, Leblanc (1998) observed a rate of 25% (3 out of 12) with the final three-choice forms. That ratio corresponds closely to the 3.1 average of self-nominations observed in Figure 3 (88/28). Thus, do not be surprised if you notice many more self-nominations (in fact three times as many) than talent-level (15+ or top three) item scores. The incidence of self-nominations varies greatly from item to item, with the abilities that are most difficult to observe, especially social abilities, giving rise to more of them. There are also significant gender differences, as well as differences in incidence according to rank: their percentage decreases slightly from the first to the third rank (see chapter 5).

b. *Validity of self-nominations*. As pointed out in chapter 1 (see also chapter 5), our research has confirmed that, notwithstanding their large number, self-nominations do not affect the *reliability* of the peer scores. But, that large incidence level casts a dark shadow on their validity. If 35% or so of the students consider themselves to be among the top 10–15% of their peers on any typical ability, a majority of them have to be wrong, no doubt about that. Only in Lake Wobegon do we find all students to be above average! The problem with that over-abundance of self-nominations is that the administration procedure does not allow students to take a second look at them and to remove the more doubtful. Moreover, while a rate of 35% of self-nominations is clearly exaggerated in the case of most students, it will sometimes reflect quite accurately—and even underestimate (see student 13 in Figure 7)—peer and teacher judgments. In a nutshell, we have found no way to reduce their number except through the specific directions given when **Tracking Talents** is administered.

Yet, self-nominations correlate as well on average with peer scores as do teacher nominations; there are no major differences globally between the two sets of correlations (Massé & Gagné, 1996). What is interesting is that the self versus peer correlations are higher at the junior high level, whereas it is the teacher versus peer correlations that are a bit higher at the elementary level. Keep in mind that these correlations are generally modest: most range between .30 and .55, which confirms the complementary role of these three sources of information about students' abilities.

In order to have a more hands-on view of the limited validity of self-nominations, just compare their number in Figure 7 with the number of moderate scores (15+); you will observe very different patterns. For example, some students are very modest: they name themselves rarely while they are perceived as talented in many fields (e.g., students 13 and 16). Others are just the opposite: they enter numerous self-nominations that remain unrequited in terms of peer or teacher choices (e.g., students 4, 10, 14, and 28). In many cases, the frequencies closely match, but we would need to verify if the self-nominated items correspond to the talent-level peer scores of that student. Look, for instance, at student 15 who received six 15+ peer scores and named herself six times also (see items 2, 3, 6, 8, 9, and 12 in the Figure 3 Data Sheet). Except for item 3 (Comedian), where her peer score was only the sixth highest, she was right on target since she obtained one of the three top peer scores for the five other items (see Figure 7). Moreover, five of her six self-nominations corresponded to teacher choices (except item 2).

c. *How to use self-nominations.* Because of their large number, we do not recommend that you mark in the Score Sheet all the self-nominations that were highlighted in the Data Sheet. Not only would it take more than half an hour do to so and produce a dangerous "overdose" of marks on the Score Sheet, but, more importantly, that information would be useless in too many cases. Indeed, if it were already clear from peer and teacher data that the student's abilities in a particular domain are outstanding, the presence or absence of a self-nomination would have little influence on a selection decision. Similarly, if both peer and teacher data indicated no special ability, the presence of a self-nomination would have little impact (except, maybe, if it were the only one made by that student).

Self-nominations become interesting in doubtful cases, either when the peers and the teacher disagree on the top scorers or when both sources place a particular student in a group of borderline cases. For example, notice in Figure 7 that student 10 gave herself seven self-nominations and received five teacher choices, four of them without any peer support, and one associated with a borderline peer score of 13 for item 6 (Lightning). The fact that student 10 named herself for that item could reinforce, along with the teacher choice, the significance of that borderline score, and suggest a closer examination of that student's academic talents. No doubt users will find many other ways to compare these three sources of information.

D - Special Applications

Tracking Talents will be used mostly for selection purposes. In that particular context, data will be gathered from various sources and merged one way or another to facilitate the decision process. Usually, participating teachers and students will not have access to the *Tracking Talents* results. The suggestions below aim at modifying that standard procedure by proposing new applications and goals for *Tracking Talents*. Please keep in mind that these are ideas that were proposed by team members during the years of Project PAIRS; most have not been tried yet.

a. *A social awareness building tool.* The teacher could present the instrument to her students, discussing with them what to look for in each domain when trying to identify the more talented. While that task is easy for some abilities (e.g., academic or physical), others probably require a much keener sense of observation and good guidelines, especially social abilities. With some abilities (e.g., Handyman, Musician, Dancer), students will have to gather knowledge that is not readily available in the school environment. After that discussion, the students could complete the form, then keep it for a few days as they examine the behavior of their peers more attentively. They could even compare their choices with each other and discuss the reasons for discrepancies. The teacher could also propose a group activity in which students would describe their achievements in a particular domain, so that peers could build a better picture of individual differences in achievement.

b. *A tool for curriculum differentiation.* Teachers could apply their knowledge of the students' special abilities to daily learning activities in the classroom. For instance, they could group students with similar talents and have them work on a long-term project related to that area of talent. At other times, they could distribute students with a similar talent (e.g., creativity) into different clusters, so that their special expertise could benefit the problem-solving activities in these groups. No doubt that other uses will emerge as *Tracking Talents* becomes disseminated in more school districts.

c. *A tool to improve self-esteem.* *Tracking Talents* is particularly interesting because it widens the concept of talent well beyond the traditional academic talents rewarded in schools. If the results are shown to the students, many of those who do not belong to the select group of academic high achievers will discover that they appear among the top three or four best (as judged by their peers and/or teacher) in at least one ability or subgroup; that could bolster their self-esteem and make the teacher realize with more acuity that many of her students are perceived as possessing special talents. It would be a good occasion to point out that all talents should be valued and recognized, and that academic success is not the only goal worth pursuing or rewarding. On the other hand, teachers should keep in mind that approximately half of her students will *not* appear even once on average among the top performers. Therefore, they should watch for indices of major disappointment among the unchosen, especially when so many will have been recognized for their special achievements.

d. *A tool to explore talent development.* Over the years, many teachers and coordinators of enrichment programs have mentioned that it was very easy to teach the basics of the Differentiated Model of Giftedness and Talent (see Appendix A) to young students. With appropriate examples, each of the five components (gifts, intrapersonal and environmental catalysts, chance, LTP) can be easily understood, as long as one does not expect indepth understanding of the complex interactions between them. It might be a worthwhile enrichment—even whole-group—activity to present the DMGT and ask talented students to explain how it applies to their own situations. Different students could compare similarities and differences in the relative importance of the various components as they apply them to their own cases. It might even be possible to look at differences between fields of talent, for instance, to compare academic programs with special arts or sports programs, in terms of enrichment possibilities, respect for individual differences in ease and pace of learning, availability of challenges for even the most talented, and so forth.

e. *Stretching the talent spectrum.* Students could look at their past achievements and describe the one(s) they consider to be their most significant (Kay, 1998). These could then be categorized using the **Tracking Talents** items or subgroups. Some teachers might discover areas that are not sampled by the present two forms, nor by the experimental items that were deleted as a result of the psychometric analyses performed within Project PAIRS (see Appendix B).

f. *Customizing Tracking Talents.* Both forms A and B, the items as well as their structure, are copyrighted. Therefore, creating "personal" forms by combining some of these items would be a breach of that copyright. On the other hand, nothing prevents teachers or program coordinators from creating complementary forms that could be administered with either Form A or B. These customized forms could include some of the deleted items (see Appendix B) or newly written items that tap areas overlooked by the Project PAIRS team. For instance, if one is interested in screening potential underachievers, two items from the initial pool (Spark and Flickerer) would be very helpful.

g. *Grade-wide use.* Even though we recommend *within*-group use of **Tracking Talents**, which means limiting choices to members of a self-contained group of students, *between*-group uses can be considered in some special circumstances. For instance, a teacher in Minnesota had four groups of junior high students who had been together since kindergarten. She was convinced that anyone of them knew all of the others well enough to be able to pick the best within that large cohort of 90+ students. She also believed (correctly) that such a large pool of judges would produce more reliable scores. She made some adaptations, and it worked perfectly. For example, the larger the comparison group, the more choices should be requested; with just three choices, only three or four students will clearly stand out, and in a group of 100, we would want a larger number of top performers. So, she requested four or five choices to produce a more differentiated set of top rankings. Moreover, with more choices, the nomination form and the Data Sheet needed to be redesigned. Those who are brave enough to explore that far from the beaten path will no doubt find ways to make the necessary adaptations.

A Request for Feedback

This is the first edition of the ***Tracking Talents*** User's Manual. We hope that you will find—or have found already—your experience with this instrument an interesting and rewarding one. We are aware that this manual is far from perfect, and the need for improvements will soon become apparent. Users are the best source of feedback on the usefulness of such instruments. If you find any problems with this text—omissions, obscure descriptions of procedures, or inappropriate suggestions—please write to the author at the address below. Please also write to describe any original application of ***Tracking Talents***.

Dr. Françoys Gagné
c/o Prufrock Press
P.O. Box 8813
Waco, Texas 76714
Fax: (800) 240-0333
E-Mail: Gagne@prufrock.com

Chapter Five

❈ ❈

The Research Behind Tracking Talents

This chapter serves as a brief technical manual for the ***Tracking Talents*** PTSNFs. It summarizes the research activities pursued during the life of Project PAIRS, as well as the major psychometric results obtained through three large data collections. Its structure was inspired by the guidelines proposed in *Standards for Educational and Psychological Testing* (American Psychological Association, 1985).

Because of the qualitative use of the ***Tracking Talents*** results, many precisions mentioned as essential or very desirable in the *Standards* were not judged relevant in the present context (e.g., standard errors of measurement, precise norms). Other information could not be included for lack of empirical data (e.g., concurrent validity indices); these will be noted in the text.

The chapter does not duplicate the detailed articles already published; it just reports their major observations. Interested readers will have to consult these sources. Unfortunately, much of the information was made available to professionals in education in the form of French-written master's theses, presentations at French-language scientific conferences, or unpublished technical reports. When relevant, efforts were made in this chapter to report these "foreign" studies in more detail.

A - The Experimental Instruments

One of the initial goals of Project PAIRS was to create peer nomination forms that would cover as large a spectrum of abilities as could be observed in groups of elementary and junior-high students, the primary targets for these instruments. That goal guided our search for relevant abilities to be assessed (contents), as well as the format specifications appropriate for that target population.

1. The contents

a. *Creating a database of abilities.* The database of potential abilities to be assessed was constructed from: (a) items in more than 20 existing PNFs found in the literature, (b) abilities mentioned in various taxonomies, and (c) abilities mentioned by students in preliminary interviews done in the schools with small groups of students. Over 400 items of information were categorized using the Differentiated Model of Giftedness and Talent (see Appendix A). The DMGT's four aptitude domains (intellectual, creative, socioaffective, sensorimotor) were adopted. Because, at the time, its author had proposed no classification of talent fields (Gagné, 1985), five temporary categories were created by examining the contents of the database: academic, mech/tech, artistic, interpersonal, and athletic. From that large *ability database*, over 100 different descriptions were written; they became the *item database.*

b. *Selecting the item pool.* The content validity of the item database was assessed with five different criteria (Gagné, 1989).
   - *Relevance*: Which items do not belong to abilities (e.g., motivation, personality traits)?
   - *Redundancy*: Are some items such close synonyms that they measure the same ability?
   - *Exhaustivity*: Does the item database cover all the important abilities that students manifest?
   - *Specificity*: How detailed should the items be (e.g., specific instruments in music, specific subject matters in school, or specific athletic activities)?
   - *Organization*: How should these abilities be categorized?

This last criterion generated the most heated discussions within the research team, especially when it came to choosing between a domain of giftedness and a related field of talent. This was particularly true for the creativity domain. Our own (limited!) creativity had produced only two items, all other suggestions corresponding to the manifestation of that aptitude in a particular field of talent (see the descriptions of Handyman, Craftsperson, Writer, Comedian, and Life-of-the-party in Appendix B). The distinction between socioaffective aptitudes and interpersonal talents turned out to be the most difficult to operationalize. We finally considered as aptitudes items that described general interpersonal abilities, such as counseling (Guardian angel/Counselor), empathy (Confidant), and support of others (Cheerleader/Stimulator).

In the case of physical activities, the interviews conducted with students revealed how rich and diverse talents in athletics and sports were. Rather than favor some sports over others, we opted to cover a few general aptitudes: speed, strength, flexibility, agility, and endurance (see Appendix B). At the end of that analysis, 40 different items remained; one of them (Spark) did not assess an ability, but the phenomenon of underachievement. The items in that experimental item pool are schematically described in Appendix B (for more details, see Gagné, Bégin, & Talbot, 1993).

Note: Two new items, Actor and Flickerer, were created between studies I and II.

2. The format

Various elements of the physical appearance and organization of the questionnaires received close attention.

1. *Presentation*. Each item was presented by means of three elements: a title, a visual symbol (icon), and a short description. These components aimed at making the task both attractive and clear.
2. *Gender neutrality*. Whenever possible, the titles were made sexually neutral; also, each description began with the words: "A [title] is a girl or a boy who ..."
3. *Number of choices*. Four nominations were requested. From an earlier tryout, we knew this number was about the maximum differentiation that students (and teachers) could make.
4. *Ranking*. It was also clear from the tryout that a first choice meant a higher level of ability than a second or a third choice. Thus, the examiner asked students to find the first best, then a second best, and so on. Ranks would be taken into consideration in the scoring system.
5. *Self-nominations*. Because of contradictory information in the literature concerning the validity of self-nominations, they were not allowed. Instead, it was decided to conduct a special study to assess their impact on the talent scores (see Study II on page 52).
6. *Answering procedure*. We decided to use a numbered class list. The students would have to find in that list the number of the chosen peer (called the Student Identification Number or SIN), then write that number on the answer sheet. That decision was based on three considerations: (a) the time it takes to write names (first and last), (b) the time-consuming coding process to prepare that information for computer entry, and (c) problems with a provincial law protecting confidential information and requesting written parental approval when seeking such information (the numbers were not judged "confidential" as long as the lists remained in the schools). Tryouts did confirm that most fourth-grade students could easily perform that task.

B - Major Data Collections

1. Study I (1988)

This first large data collection aimed at gathering as much psychometric information as possible on each of the 40 items in the initial item pool.

a. *Subjects*. The sample was composed of 2,432 French-speaking upper-elementary students, distributed about equally between genders and between grades 4, 5, and 6. The 88 groups sampled came from 17 schools in three school districts in the greater Montreal area; there were on average 28 students per group. All groups were heterogeneous in terms of abilities. Their 88 teachers were mostly women (82%).

b. *Instruments*. Three pairs of experimental forms (A1-A2, B1-B2, C1-C2) were prepared. Each form contained 12 items, four of which were common to both members of a pair. The two forms of a given pair were presented to the same subjects within a three-week interval. Thus, each student was assessed by his or her peers on 20 different abilities, twice on the four common ones. Since this arrangement provided 60 different "slots," it allowed us to insert 20 of the 40 items of the pool in two different pairs of forms, thereby enriching the analysis of the empirical groupings of the items. Each of the six forms comprised 2 two-sided sheets: one listed the 12 descriptions, six per side, and the other was the answer sheet.

c. *Procedure*. The 30 or so groups from each grade level were equally divided between six experimental conditions: three pairs and two presentation orders (e.g., A1 followed by A2, or A2 followed by A1). To maximize the knowledge that students would have of each other's abilities, the data collection was conducted in May, toward the end of the school year. There was an interval of approximately three weeks between the administration of the two PTNFs. Each questionnaire took between 25 and 35 minutes to administer, depending on the age of the students, the classroom climate, and the style of the examiner.

It was not always possible to prevent a few students from expressing some of their choices vocally; this could slightly inflate the reliability measures (inter-peer agreement) in these groups. The teacher completed the PTNF at the same time as her students. Eighty-four teachers participated in the first visit, and 67 of them were present to complete the second member of the pair. End-of-year grades in language and math were collected from all children whose parents had given proper authorization; it represented 84% of the sample.

Since order of presentation was shown not to affect the results, we were able to merge together all the students who had received a given form, about 800 students on average. We were also able to merge the results from both members of a given pair, thus obtaining 24 different talent scores for each student, four of them repeats.

d. *Verifying non-responses*. Approximately 4% of the questionnaires were discarded because of too many missing data, namely less than 16 (33%) of the 48 choices requested. Among the remaining ones, non-responses amounted to 17.5% and 19.2% respectively for the first and second data collections. Beyond individual differences (from 0% to 67%), variations in non-response rates were found to be mostly related to item content and rank of choice (Gagné, Bégin, & Talbot, 1993). For example, we observed 6.5% of non-responses for first choices and 33% for fourth choices. Similarly, non-responses ranged from 8% (Encyclopedia) to 36% (Mechanic). The non-response rate among teachers was 18% on average. Both the item content and rank effects were similar in size to those in students' copies. For instance, there were 7.5%, 12.7%, and 20.7% of non-responses on average for their first three choices.

e. *Computing the talent scores*. The choices received by each student were weighed by rank (1st = 4 points; 2nd = 3; etc.), then added for each item in a given form. These totals were then standardized on a 100-point scale, mainly to control the impact of differences in group size (see chapter 3, part C). A zero score meant that the student had received no choices at all from his or her peers for that particular item; a score of 100 meant that the student was the first choice of all his or her peers. These scores did not follow a normal distribution; 32% of the students (from 14% to 49% depending on the item) received a score of zero. The frequencies decreased rapidly as the scores increased, producing a negatively accelerated curve. Twelve percent of the students (from 8% to 16% depending on the item) received a score equal to or larger than 20 (see chapter 4, part A, Figure 8; Appendix C).

The teachers' choices were simply weighed by rank. The obtained score distributions were also negatively accelerated, but with a much larger proportion of zero scores (from 85% to 91% depending on the item, with a median of 86%).

2. Study II (1989)

This second large data collection pursued four distinct objectives: (a) assess the psychometric qualities and grouping patterns of a reduced set of items, (b) evaluate the applicability of ***Tracking Talents*** with older students, namely seventh- and eighth-grade junior high students, (c) compare choices made in same-gender classes to those in mixed-gender groups, and (d) examine the impact of self-nominations on the talent scores.

a. *Subjects.* The 1989 sample was made up of four different subsamples. The first one comprised 1,899 elementary school students and their teachers, similarly distributed with respect to gender and grade level as the previous year's sample; these students belonged to 60 groups in 12 schools of two school districts. The second subsample, distributed about equally between both genders and two grades (7 and 8), was composed of 1,215 junior high students and their teachers; these students belonged to 39 groups in four schools. The third subsample included 13 groups from a girls' high school and 13 groups from a boys' high school, for a total of 864 students. Finally, a fourth subsample was assembled to assess the impact of self-nominations; it was composed of 391 students, distributed more or less evenly by gender and grade level (grades 4 to 8), for a total of 17 groups.

b. *Instruments.* The results of various psychometric analyses performed on the first year's data guided the revision of the PTNFs. Twelve redundant or unreliable items were dropped, and two new ones were created (see Flickerer and Actor in Appendix B). The three new forms (D-1, D-2, D-3) contained a total of 30 different items, 9 to 11 per form. These three forms were less heterogeneous than those of the preceding year. The format of the new questionnaires was essentially unchanged, except that the two separate sheets were combined into a four-page booklet. The same answering technique was used, namely the transfer of a student's number from a numbered class list. A more heterogeneous fourth form (D-4) was prepared for the study of self-nominations (see Massé & Gagné, 1996).

c. *Procedure.* The administration procedure was essentially the same as in Study I, except that there was only one visit to each group.

d. *Data transformation.* Non-response rates for students and teachers were approximately the same as the year before; talent scores were computed in the same way.

3. Study III (1996)

This last data collection was conducted in the context of a master's thesis (Leblanc, 1998). Its aim was to gather reliability and validity data specific to the two final forms of ***Tracking Talents***.

a. *Subjects.* A total of 708 students from 28 groups in two partly rural school districts completed both forms; they were distributed about equally by gender and grade level (grades 5 and 6). All groups were heterogeneous in terms of academic abilities, and the boy/girl ratio exceeded 60/40 (or 40/60) in only four groups.

b. *Instruments.* The two final forms of ***Tracking Talents*** (A & B) are described in chapter 1. To assess short-term stability, two short forms of four items each (AA and BB) were created, using items from Forms A and B.

c. *Procedure*. Two 14-group subsamples were created, each receiving a different form on the first visit. The second examination was held within three weeks of the first and completed by the same examiner. Students who got the A-B sequence received form AA on the second visit, while form BB was administered to those in the B-A sequence.

The major empirical results from the three data collections of Project PAIRS are grouped according to the two traditional families of psychometric information: *reliability* and *validity*. Because teacher and self-nominations involve only one judge, thus one set of choices, they lend themselves to fewer analyses; this does not imply that these two sources offer less reliable and valid information than the peer scores. As mentioned earlier, each source has valuable information to contribute to the screening process, information that should be weighed against that of the other two sources.

C - The Reliability of Tracking Talents Scores

The concept of reliability covers all questions related to the reproducibility of scores: reproducibility when judges change, reproducibility in time, reproducibility when the format changes, and so forth. Reliability assessment precedes validity analyses for the simple reason that it constitutes a prerequisite condition of validity: unreliable measures cannot measure anything validly. We will present in this section four different sets of results associated with the reliability of peer and teacher nominations.

1. Number of choices

To what extent does the number of choices made by the students affect the reliability of the talent scores, more specifically, their precision? Theoretically, the more choices there are, the more reproducible the information will be. On the other hand, trying to discriminate among non-outstanding students might generate mostly measurement error. Practically, users appreciate instruments that are as short as possible without decreasing the quality of the information. To answer the initial question, four different scores were computed: using only the first choices, using the first two choices, and so forth. The correlations presented in Table 2 are averages obtained from an analysis of 12 different items.

As can be seen, the four scores were highly correlated, suggesting that two choices would be sufficient to rank order the students very precisely according to their level of ability as perceived by peers. Even the first choice alone is already highly correlated (.89) with a score using four choices. Of course, the fact that first choices receive 4 points gives them predominance over the lower-ranked choices, thus preserving high correlations. To be on the safe side, and considering that, even with four choices, the task was not unduly long, it was decided to maintain three choices in the final forms.

2. Inter-peer agreement (IPA)

Inter-peer agreement (IPA) is the most important type of reliability in the case of instru-

---

Table 2
Correlation Matrix (Pearson r) Between Series of Scores Computed with Different Numbers of Choices

---

Number of choices

		2	3	4
	1	.96	.93	.89
Number of choices	2		.99	.97
	3			.99

---

ments based on interpersonal judgments. A high level of IPA means that the choices of a typical judge are reproduced—almost in the same order—by a majority of the other judges. Using the 1988 data, 2,112 IPA coefficients (Cronbach's alpha) were computed, one for each item (12) in each group of students (88) from each data collection (2). In technical terms, they represent the expected degree of similarity—as measured by a correlation coefficient—between these scores and those any student in the group would obtain from other *equivalent* groups of peers. Here are the major results (for more details, see Gagné, Bégin, & Talbot, 1993).

a. The two data collections of 1988 did not differ significantly. Small differences were observed between the six forms, largely explained by the particular groups of items making up each form. The coefficients were very stable for a given item appearing in two different forms.

b. Systematic differences between groups of students were observed, some groups showing, over all items, much better IPA coefficients than others on average. That phenomenon explained approximately 15% of the variation observed among the 2,100+ alpha coefficients.

c. A small significant difference was observed between the three grade levels; the coefficients from grade 4 groups were somewhat lower (.79) on average than those from the two other grades (.83). But this factor explained only 3% of the variation among the IPA coefficients.

d. The most important observed differences were related to the type of ability measured (Content effect). This factor alone explained 39% of the variation observed on average. Means ranged from .61 for the item Confidant to .97 for the item Hercules, with an overall mean of .82. Only 9 items out of 40 had average IPA coefficients below .75, a commonly recognized minimum threshold of acceptability. Table 3 presents various types of reliability coefficients associated with the items in the two final forms. The first four columns reproduce average IPA coefficients obtained in studies I (1988), II (1989), and III (1996).

Table 3
Various Reliability Coefficients Obtained
for the 24 Items of the Two Final Forms

Item title	IPA coefficients				Stability coefficients Short-term			One-year
	1988[a]	1989el[b]	1989hs[b]	1996[c]	1988[d]	1996[c]	1988t[d]	1989[d]
Form A								
Encyclopedia	.95	.93	.88	.94		.97		.76
Handyman	.80	.74	.70	.78	.84		.57	
Comedian	.92	.94	.94	.91		.93		.76
Programmer	.84	.85	.77	.82		.93		.73
Counselor/confidant	.61	.79	.66	.73		.80		.42
Lightning	.95	--	--	.94	.96		.73	.86
Scientist	.83	.82	.68	.83	.86		.63	
Stimulator/cheerleader	.66	.74	.67	.60				
Actor	--	.85	.81	.79				
Mechanic	.73	.79	.77	.78				
Judge	.70	.60	.43	.63	.85		.47	
Bright idea	.82	.81	.79	.75	.85		.65	.44
Form B								
Hercules	.97	.93	.93	.95				.79
Musician	.89	.90	.83	.92	.92	.93	.64	.84
Leader	.85	.83	.80	.79	.88		.55	
Artist	.93	.90	.79	.95	.96	.97	.61	.76
Singer	.75	.75	.69	.78				
Sociable/diplomat	.67	.60	.58	.63		.76		.42
Spokesperson	.77	.79	.85	.87				
Tireless one	.86	.88	.86	.87		.93		
Craftsperson	.79	.81	.64	.75				
Dancer	.81	.80	.84	.83				
Speaker	.85	.91	.91	.80				
Hare	.91	.94	.90	.90				
Mean (Median)	.82	.82	.76	.82	.89	.90	.61	(.76)

[a]Reproduced from Gagné, Bégin, & Talbot, 1993, Table 1, p. 43.
[b]Reproduced from Lacasse, 1991, Table 25, p. 149.
[c]Reproduced from Leblanc, 1998, Table 3.3 (p. 32) & 3.4 (p. 40).
[d]Adapted from Gagné & Bélanger, 1994.

e. Items with low IPA coefficients came from many categories, but mostly from the socioaffective and interpersonal domains.

f. As shown in Table 3, very similar results were obtained with the 1989 sample, at both the elementary (1989el) and the high school (1989hs) levels (see Lacasse, 1991), and also with the 1996 sample (see Leblanc, 1998).

3. Stability indices

a. *Short-term stability indices.* The term *stability* refers to the reproducibility of measures over time, either short periods of less than two to three months or longer periods of one year or more. Short-term stability was assessed in studies I and III with five groups of four items—three groups in 1988 and two in 1996—who were common to both members of each pair of questionnaires. The two series of results appear in Table 3 (columns 5 and 6). In Study I, the correlations between the pairs of scores ranged from .84 to .96, with a mean of .89; in Study III, the range was .76 to .97, with a mean of .90. Only two items (Musician and Artist) were used in both studies, and the results are remarkably similar. Notice the very strong relationship between IPA and stability coefficients even though the two sources of error are qualitatively distinct—time versus persons. The ranking of items from best to worse is approximately the same in all columns of Table 3, which confirms the importance of content (the nature of the ability assessed) in explaining differences in reliability.

b. *Long-term stability indices.* Correlating scores one year apart is as much a validity problem as a reliability problem, since real changes may have happened in the interval between the two examinations (Anastasi & Urbina, 1997); lower values are to be expected. To assess long-term stability, Forms A-1 and A-2 were readministered one year later to a few groups of students in which were present students from the preceding year's sample (Gagné & Bélanger, 1994). About 40% of the judges were in the same group the year before, and almost 90% were in the same school.

This means that we were assessing simultaneously three potential sources of change: (a) changes in judgment over time by the same judges, (b) IPA, and (c) real behavior changes by the students being rated one year later. Analyzed over 20 different items, the stability coefficients ranged from .38 (Confidant) to .89 (Calculator), with a median of .77 (see Table 3, column 8, for a few examples). The IPA average for that group of 20 items was .90, a level somewhat higher than in studies I and II for that group of items (Gagné, Bégin, & Talbot, 1993). Again, the two series of coefficients were very closely related (see Table 3).

c. *Stability of teacher and self-nominations.* Although agreement between judges is irrelevant here, the stability of the judgments over time should be assessed. In the case of teachers, the short-term (three weeks) stability of their choices was evaluated with the Study I data, in which 67 teachers had completed both members of a pair of forms (Gagné & Bélanger, 1994). As shown in column 7 (1988t) of Table 3, the stability coefficients were significantly lower, mostly due to the fact that they were based on only one judge. The stability of self-nominations was not assessed.

D - The Validity of Tracking Talents Scores

The implicit question behind all validity analyses is: To what extent do these scores represent accurately the individuals' "real" status on the trait measured? Do score differences on any item, whether from peer, teacher, or self-nominations, closely approximate real ability differences between these students? We will briefly describe below six different sets of empirical data that bear directly on the validity of the **Tracking Talents** scores.

1. Self-nominations

At the beginning of Project PAIRS, we were worried that if these young students were allowed to nominate themselves they might overdo it, thus lowering the validity of the scores, not only because of their self-choices, but also because they would not be naming the students who really deserved to be chosen. This is why self-nominations were not permitted in study I, but became the object of a special parallel data collection within Study II.

We looked for three specific types of information in that special part of Study II: (a) descriptive information about self-nominations, namely their incidence, as well as any rate fluctuations according to various variables (e.g., type of talent assessed, age and sex of students, rank of choice, etc.); (b) the impact of their presence on the reliability of the talent scores, especially inter-peer agreement; and (c) the relationship between self-nominations and those from peers and teachers. We have summarized below the more important results (see also Massé, 1992; Massé & Gagné, 1996).

a. The average number of self-nominations was 5.2; it corresponds to an incidence of 43%. The full range of 0 to 12 was utilized, but two-thirds of the students named themselves between two and seven times. Boys used them more often than girls (5.47 vs. 4.89). When students name themselves, they are in fact saying: "I consider myself to be among the four best of the group in this ability domain." The best four in a group of 26 or 27 correspond to a rate of emergence of approximately 15%. But, the average rate of self-nominations was just over 40%, almost three times higher!

   Similar results were obtained with the 1996 data. But, since only three choices were requested, the rate of self-nominations dropped to 25% in both forms, with approximately 84% of the students distributed almost equally between frequencies zero to five. So, on average, there were close to three self-nominations in either form (A = 2.9; B = 3.2), again, many more than talent-level peer scores.

b. First-rank self-nominations were somewhat more frequent; the rate went down slightly from rank to rank. But, this tendency interacted with gender: boys used the first ranks slightly more often than girls, while girls tended to put their own name in third or fourth place more often than boys.

c. Self-nominations varied extensively depending on the talent assessed. Percentages ranged from 30% (Grammar book) to 50% (Gymnast).

d. There was also an important interaction between content and gender: Boys named themselves more often than girls on items Comedian, Hare, Handyman, Scientist, and Encyclopedia, while girls had a higher rate of self-nominations on item Musician. As will be seen below (section 5: Gender orientation), with only one exception (Encyclopedia), these gender differences paralleled the peer judgments quite well.

e. There was a slight downward trend in the rate of self-nominations from grade 4 to grade 8, mostly at the extremes, namely very low and very high frequencies. But, important variations between groups within each grade attenuated the importance of that age effect.

f. We computed an IPA (inter-peer agreement) coefficient (Cronbach's alpha) for each item within each group of students, either with self-nominations included or recoded as missing data. There was no significant difference for any item. With hindsight, it is easy to see why: a self-nomination adds only one choice to the student's score. If he or she is named by a majority of his/her peers, that additional choice will not change the resulting score by much. If, on the other hand, the student receives no peer choices, that single self-nomination will give him or her a score of 3 or 4 at best on the 100-point scale used for peer talent scores.

g. Self-nominations were correlated with peer and teacher nominations for each item on a samplewide basis (n = 391). The correlations with peer scores were moderate (.44) on average, somewhat higher (.54) with the junior high subgroup than the elementary one (.41); as usual, item content strongly influenced these correlations. The correlations between self and teacher nominations were much lower, with an average of .23 over the 12 items. But, this was attributed in large part to the fact that we were comparing two sets of single judgments, a situation similar to comparing the choices of two student judges or comparing the performance of students on two items from an achievement test. In such cases, correlations cannot be high because of measurement error. This confirms the positive impact on reliability of creating group scores.

In conclusion, because self-nominations had no adverse effect on the talent scores, and because students always ask to be allowed to use them, we decided that self-nominations would be permitted in any future use of **Tracking Talents**.

2. Friendships and nominations

In the context of peer nominations, friendships pose a problem similar to that of self-nominations: Students might be tempted too often to name their best friend irrespective of that student's real abilities, thus jeopardizing to some degree the validity of the peer scores. Since it was not possible to prevent such best friend choices, we tried to assess the impact of that particular behavior by first asking students to identify their best friend's SIN, and then looking at (a) the incidence of their presence among the nominations; (b) potential differences associated with age, gender, and item content; and (c) their impact on the talent scores. Here are some results from unpublished analyses of that information (Gagné, 1992, 1993b).

a. Fifty-eight percent of the students were named at least once as best friend; but, just a few (5%) were named more than twice. Only 44% of the choices were reciprocal, a little bit more among girls (46.5%) than boys (41.5%).

b. There were no overall gender differences in frequency of choice, but a powerful gender bias was observed: 96.4% of the girls chose girls, while 93.5% of the boys chose boys.

c. Among the choices made for the 12 items of a given form, the best friend appeared 4.3 times on average, in decreasing frequency from the first (1.77) to the fourth (.60) rank. That incidence level means that the identified best friend was named about once every three items. That ratio of 36% is just a bit smaller than the average incidence of self-nominations mentioned above (43%). Only 7% of the students did not name their best friend at all.

    Note: That incidence level would probably be significantly lower with the final forms, since there are only three choices instead of four.

d. The items where best friend nominations most frequently appeared were: Confidant (66%), Cheerleader (48%), Diplomat (47%), Bright idea (43%), and Quick wrist (43%). The lowest percentage was 25% (Spark).

e. The frequent presence of the best friends as choices had no perceptible impact on the reliability and validity of the peer scores. Scores computed with or without best friend choices were correlated .987 on average. Again, in hindsight, that result is not at all surprising since the explanation given for the lack of impact of self-nominations on peer scores (see paragraph 1.f on page 59) applies perfectly here, as well.

f. Whereas birds of a feather flock together, best friends' patterns of abilities do not seem to overlap much: There was just a slight tendency for students to choose as best friends those who were more similar to them in terms of their abilities. The tendency was more pronounced in the case of reciprocal choices; it also varied depending on the item, in interaction with the gender of the subjects. Reciprocal best friends appeared somewhat more similar in socioaffective and physical abilities than in intellectual and academic ones. Gagné (1993b) observed:

    It is clear from these data that there is little tendency for these best achievers to become close friends. The problem is compounded by the overwhelming sex bias in friendship choices. This effect guarantees that if the two highest achievers are not of the same sex, they will not choose each other. The most interesting finding in this study is the role played by other abilities as criteria for friendship ties. Socioaffective abilities emerged as criteria for both boys and girls. This is not surprising, considering the nature of friendships.... In conclusion, these results would lead to the following answer to the title question: "Yes, birds of a feather do flock together to a certain degree, as long as the feather is not intellectual or academic! (p. 3)

3. The dimensions of talents

From the beginning of Project PAIRS, we were very curious to see what kinds of groupings would emerge from the peer and teacher choices, and, more specifically, to what extent the DMGT's ability categories would be confirmed by empirical clusterings within these large databases. Recall that we used six different forms in Study I to maximize combinations of various groups and pairs of items. We chose to search for groupings using the technique of exploratory principal components analysis (Tabachnick & Fidell, 1989).

Analyses were performed with the three major databases, first with the whole sample and then separately for the scores of boys and girls (Talbot, 1991). In the case of Study I, three factor analyses were performed, each done on the data from the two members of a given pair of forms (A1-A2, B1-B2, C1-C2). Twenty different scores were thus used in each case. Three other analyses were computed with the three 1989 forms (for more details, see Gagné & Talbot, 1995). Finally, another trio of analyses (total sample, boys, girls) was computed with the Study III data (Leblanc, 1998). Here are the major observations from these analyses.

a. The 1988 and 1989 analyses confirmed the presence of eight somewhat stable groups of items: (a) academic talents, (b) mechanical/technical talents, (c) physical aptitudes, (d) interpersonal/affective abilities, (e) musical talent, (f) talent in visual arts, (g) talent in drama/entertainment, and (h) underachievement.

b. Factor analyses were computed using the teacher scores from the 1988 data collection. The groupings were very similar to those obtained with the peer scores (Gagné & Talbot, 1995).

c. The most relevant factor analyses are those performed with the two final forms of **Tracking Talents**. Table 4 on page 62, reproduced from Leblanc (1998), shows the results of the analysis done with the total sample of 708 students using the combined information of both Forms A and B. Six of the eight groupings created for the final forms (see Table 1) clearly appeared as factors: (a) academic talents, (b) interpersonal abilities, (c) physical abilities, (d) mechanical/technical talents, (e) arts-drama, and (f) visual arts. As shown in Table 4, the three items of the musical subgroup (Form B) remained separated, with two of them distantly related to interpersonal abilities. Also, our subdivision of interpersonal abilities into two areas (ethical/affective vs. social influence) was not perceived by the students; the whole area remained more or less undifferentiated.

d. Small but significant differences were observed when the factor analyses were computed separately for boys and girls. For example, the interpersonal factor is much stronger in the girls' data, while the reverse is true for the mechanical/technical factor (Talbot, 1991; Leblanc, 1998).

e. The subgroup scores are not based on the factor loadings, but on the averaging of item scores (see chapter 3, part C.4). Since the various abilities tend to be slightly correlated, moderate correlations between the subgroup scores should be expected. Table 5 on page 71 presents the correlation matrix between the eight subgroup scores and two total scores from Forms A and B.

If we examine the Form A and B correlations separately, it is clear that the two pairs of four subgroup scores are slightly or moderately correlated; only the PH score in Form B shows almost null correlations with the other subgroups within its form. Yet, these PH scores are slightly correlated with the subgroup scores in Form A. Similarly, the vast majority of the subgroup scores in Form A entertain low to moderate correlations with the subgroup scores in Form B. Note also how strong the correlations of the social influence

Table 4
Factor Loadings on the Six Significant Factors
of a Principal Components Analysis (1996 Sample)[a]

Item title	1	2	3	4	5	6
Encyclopedia	92					
Lightning	87					
Speaker	67				48	
Scientist	66			56		
Programmer	60			45		
Bright idea	56	51			34	
Musician	38					
Judge		83				
Stimulator/cheerleader		74	35			
Counselor/confidant	52	66				
Sociable/diplomat	34	66				
Dancer		62				
Leader	43	54	37		34	
Singer		53			46	
Tireless one			91			
Hare			91			
Hercules			65			
Mechanic				90		
Handyman				87		30
Actor					74	
Comedian			44		73	
Spokesperson	47	41			49	
Artist						88
Craftsperson						79
% of explained variance	17.8	15.9	11.5	9.4	9.2	7.4

[a]Reproduced from Leblanc, 1998, Table 3.5, p. 43.

subgroup are with both academic talent and socioaffective abilities. These mostly significant correlations between the subgroups (the positive manifold mentioned in chapter 4, part B.4) confirm the construct validity of the MT scores.

This network of relationships might have been artificially intensified to some degree by a halo effect, which would bring students who show some degree of multitalent to be chosen for other abilities when no one seems to emerge clearly.

Table 5
Correlation Matrix for the Eight Subgroup Scores
and Two Total Scores of Forms A and B[a]

	ME	DR	AF	MT.A	PH	MU	VI	SO	MT.B
AC ademic	.47	.23	.45	.89	.06	.35	.33	.67	.56
ME ch./tech.		.13	.06	.65	.17	.02	.24	.22	.26
DR ama			.22	.50	.32	.27	.16	.53	.54
AF fective (Socio-)				.59	.14	.50	.24	.66	.61
MT score A					.21	.40	.37	.76	.70
PH ysical						-.07	-.02	.20	.55
MU sic							.28	.50	.61
VI sual arts								.30	.52
SO cial influence									.82

[a]Computed from Leblanc's (1998) database.

---

4. Peers versus teachers

Some psychometricians consider that the strength of the relationships between peer and teacher scores contributes to our knowledge of the reliability of the ***Tracking Talents*** scores; are we not comparing agreement between judges, just as we did with IPA coefficients? On the other hand, others will consider that the comparison of two distinct sources of information comes more appropriately under the subject of convergent validity (Anastasi & Urbina, 1997); comparing sources becomes a form of cross-validation. As shown by the position of this section, we adopted that second point of view. Cardinal (1991) examined the relationships between peer and teacher scores from various viewpoints using data from Study I. Here are her major observations.

a. The average peer-teacher correlation was a moderate .52 (see Table 6, column 1 on page 64). This might be judged low for measures of agreement between judges, especially if we compare them to IPA coefficients. But, it should be recalled that the teacher "scores" not only are just four ranked choices plus a lot of zeros for all the non-nominated, but are also the judgments of a single individual.

b. Moreover, teachers are not always in a very good position to assess abilities that are rarely exhibited in the school environment (e.g., Handyman, Dancer, Salesperson). Indeed, as in other analyses already presented, the item content strongly influenced the peer-teacher

Table 6
Various Validity Coefficients
Related to the 24 Items in the Final Two Forms

Item title			Correlation with grades[a]	
	P vs T[a]	Gender orient. (% G)[b]	peers	teachers
Form A				
Encyclopedia	.68	-- (43)	.56	.34
Handyman	.52	BB (18)	.22	.16
Comedian	.46	BB (18)	-.04	.04
Programmer	.67	BB (22)	.32	.21
Counselor/confidant	.35	GG (73)	.40	.20
Lightning	.72	-- (51)	.57	.46
Scientist	.58	BB (23)	.34	.23
Stimulator/cheerleader	.38	-- (56)	.27	.21
Actor	--	-- (45)	--	--
Mechanic	.47	BB (07)	.08	-.03
Judge	.42	-- (52)	.36	.22
Bright idea	.48	-- (52)	.42	.24
Form B				
Hercules	.69	BB (08)	-.08	-.08
Musician	.65	GG (77)	.40	.21
Leader	.52	-- (46)	.32	.21
Artist	.58	-- (51)	.19	.01
Singer	.38	GG (80)	.21	.08
Sociable/diplomat	.43	G (58)	.43	.21
Spokesperson	.57	-- (53)	.36	.30
Tireless one	.34	BB (17)	.00	-.09
Craftsperson	.49	G (59)	.30	.11
Dancer	.50	GG (87)	.10	.12
Speaker	.57	-- (54)	.41	.31
Hare	.41	BB (26)	.02	-.05
Mean	.52		.27	.16

[a]Reproduced from Cardinal, 1991, Appendix C, pp. 104–105.
[b]Reproduced from Gagné, 1993c, Table 2, p.73. (B = boys; G = girls)

correlations. The leftmost column in Table 6 shows averages of peer-teacher correlations reproduced from Cardinal (1991). The percentages in that column reveal that the strongest relationships came from items Lightning (.72), Hercules (.69), Encyclopedia (.68), Programmer (.67), and Musician (.65). Among the items with the weakest peer-teacher correlations were Tireless one (.34), Confidant (.35), Stimulator (.38), and Singer (.38). This content effect explained on average 42% of the variation observed between the correlation coefficients; it indicates a very powerful variable.

c. There was also a significant—but small—overall grade level effect, explaining on average 5.5% of the variation. It indicated a slightly stronger relationship between peer and teacher scores in grade 5 (.54) and grade 6 (.53) than in grade 4 (.49).

d. Finally, Cardinal (1991) found a strong correlation (.75) between the peer-teacher correlations and the IPA coefficients: When an item generates high agreement among students, it also tends to generate high agreement between students and teachers, and vice versa.

5. Gender orientation of abilities

We discovered that a majority of the items were gender-typed. The second column in Table 6 gives the average percentages of boys among the three highest scorers as seen by peers as well as teachers from the databases of studies I and II (see Gagné, 1993c). The percentages in that column reveal that the students judged to be among the three best (top 12% or so) in their group by their peers were mostly boys in the case of items Mechanic (93% boys), Hercules (92%), Comedian (82%), and others, while girls were named much more often for items Confidant (73%), Dancer (87%), Singer (80%), and Musician (77%). These gender orientations of the various items were confirmed by looking at three different samples of peer scores, as well as three independent samples of teacher scores. Gagné (1995a) also observed that there is a gender bias in the nominations: Boys name proportionnately more boys in the case of the "male" items, and vice versa for girls.

This series of analyses brought Gagné (1993c) to conclude the following about the validity of gender differences in abilities:

All in all, the large number of gender differences, the strength of most of these differences, their reappearance in sample after sample, the support of the literature for many of them, and the very close relationship between the rankings of teachers and pupils, associated with the fact that most teachers were professional women—a group recognized as particularly sensitized to gender stereotyping—, bring us to conclude that these gender ratios represent real differences in the abilities manifested by boys and girls in the school environment. (p. 76)

6. Indices of concurrent validity

a. *A methodological challenge.* Assessing the concurrent and predictive validity of the **Tracking Talents** scores represents the biggest challenge in the psychometric study of this instrument. These two types of validity require criterion measurements to which the scores—peer, teacher, as well as self—will be compared. Since each item measures an ability that is partially independant from the others, we need to gather data on at least 24 different criterion measures, not a small task. These could range, for example, from IQ scores (Lightning) and school grades (Encyclopedia, Scientist); assessment of computer knowledge and proficiency (Programmer); all the way to parental testimony of accomplishments with tools (Handyman, Mechanic); recognized achievements in music (Musician), singing (Singer), or dance (Dancer), preferably from a specialist teacher in these domains; running times for the 200- or 400-yard dash (Hare) or for longer distances (Tireless one); and so forth.

b. *School grades as a criterion.* During the life of Project PAIRS, we were able to assess concurrent validity with just school achievement. As part of Study I, we obtained end-of-year cumulative school grades, with students in each group identified by their SIN; these grades were compared to all the peer and teacher scores in that particular database (Cardinal, 1991). The two rightmost columns in Table 6 contain the correlation coefficients of the peer and teacher scores with the school grades of 1,970 students (84% of the total sample) from the Study I sample. These correlations show that peer scores on the academic items were more closely related to end-of-year grades than teacher scores. But, that difference was judged to be an artifact produced by the lower reliability of the teacher scores. Keep in mind that peer scores average 25 or so individual judgments, while teacher scores result from only one set of judgments. Any teacher knows that it is much more precise and valid to assess math achievement with 50 questions than with just one, however good that single question might be!

E - Conclusion

This survey of the psychometric information gathered by the Project PAIRS team shows very encouraging results as well as information that invites caution in the interpretative process. Space does not allow a full discussion of the interpretative impact of all psychometric information. This is why we recommended at the beginning of chapter 4 that the use and interpretation of **Tracking Talents** be supervised by a professional well-versed in testing matters. That person should be able to extract from this chapter many additional cautionary notes besides those we have included here and there in chapters 3, 4, and 5. As questions arise during the interpretation process, some of them might find their answer in one section or the other of this chapter.

Again, aware that this manual does not answer all questions, we invite users to communicate to the author any technical questions that appear unanswered (see address at the end of chapter 4).

References

American Psychological Association (1985). *Standards for educational and psychological tests*. Washington, DC: Author.

Anastasi, A., & Urbina, S. (1997). *Psychological testing* (7th ed.). Upper Saddle River, NJ: Prentice-Hall.

Borland, J. H. (1989). *Planning and implementing programs for the gifted*. New York: Teachers College Press.

Cardinal, M. (1991). *Comparaison des désignations effectuées par des élèves et leur enseignant pour le dépistage d'enfants doués et talentueux de niveau primaire* [Comparison of the nominations made by students and teachers for the screening of gifted and talented elementary school students]. Unpublished master's thesis, Université du Québec à Montréal, Montréal, Canada.

Clark, B. (1996). *Growing up gifted* (3rd ed.). Columbus, OH: Charles E. Merrill.

Cox, J., Daniel, N., & Boston, B. O. (1985). *Educating able learners: Programs and promising practices*. Austin, TX : University of Texas Press.

Davis, G. A., & Rimm, S. B. (1989). *Education of the gifted and talented* (2nd ed.). Englewood Cliffs, NJ: Prentice-Hall.

DeHaan, R. G., & Havighurst, R. J. (1957). *Educating the gifted*. Chicago: University of Chicago Press.

Delisle, J. R. (1985). Vocational problems. In J. Freeman (Ed), *The psychology of gifted children* (pp. 367–378). Toronto, Canada: Wiley.

Delisle, J., Gubbins, E. J., Ciabotti, P., Salvatore, L., & Rucker, S. (1984). *The Muffs: Peer Identification Instrument*. New York: Trillium Press.

Gagné, F. (1985). Giftedness and talent: Reexamining a reexamination of the definitions. *Gifted Child Quarterly, 29,* 103–112.

Gagné, F. (1989). Peer nominations as a psychometric instrument: Many questions asked but few answered. *Gifted Child Quarterly, 33,* 53–58.

Gagné, F. (1991). Toward a differentiated model of giftedness and talent. In N. Colangelo & G. A. Davis (Eds.) *Handbook of gifted education* (pp. 65–80). Boston: Allyn and Bacon.

Gagné, F. (1992, November). *Friendships and peer nominations of the gifted and talented.* Paper presented at the 39th NAGC annual convention in Los Angeles.

Gagné, F. (1993a). Constructs and models pertaining to exceptional human abilities. In K. A. Heller, F. J. Mönks, & A. H. Passow (Eds.), *International handbook of research and development of giftedness and talent* (pp. 69–87). Oxford: Pergamon Press.

Gagné, F. (1993b, August). *Do birds of a feather flock together? - Sex differences in the patterns of abilities of best friends in elementary schools.* Paper presented at the 10th World

Conference on Gifted and Talented Children in Toronto, Canada.

Gagné, F. (1993c). Sex differences in the aptitudes and talents of children, as judged by peers and teachers. *Gifted Child Quarterly, 37,* 69–77.

Gagné, F. (1994). Are teachers really poor talent dectectors? Comments on Pegnato and Birch's (1959) study of the effectiveness and efficiency of various identification techniques. *Gifted Child Quarterly, 38,* 124–126.

Gagné, F. (1995a). *Characteristics and impact of sex bias in peer nominations of the gifted and talented.* GIREDT Technical Report, Department of Psychology, Université du Québec à Montréal.

Gagné, F. (1995b). From giftedness to talent: A developmental model and its impact on the language of the field. *Roeper Review, 18,* 103–111.

Gagné, F. (1998a). A proposal for subcategories within the gifted or talented populations. *Gifted Child Quarterly, 42,* 87–95.

Gagné, F. (1998b). The prevalence of gifted, talented, and multitalented individuals: Estimates from peer and teacher nominations. In R. C. Friedman & K. B. Rogers (Eds.), *Talent in context: Historical and social perspectives on giftedness* (pp. 101–126). Washington, DC: American Psychological Association.

Gagné, F., & Bélanger, J. (1994). *The stability of peer and teacher nominations of the gifted and talented.* GIREDT Technical Report, Department of Psychology, Université du Québec à Montréal.

Gagné, F., & Talbot, L. (1995). *Comparison of the factor structures extracted from peer and teacher nominations of the gifted and talented.* GIREDT Technical Report, Department of Psychology, Université du Québec à Montréal.

Gagné, F., Bégin, J., & Talbot, L. (1993). How well do peers agree among themselves when nominating the gifted and talented? *Gifted Child Quarterly, 37,* 39–45.

Gallagher, J. J. (1985). *Teaching the gifted child* (3rd ed.). Boston: Allyn & Bacon.

Gardner, H. (1983). *Frames of mind: The theory of multiple intelligences.* New York: Basic Books.

Hoge, R. D., & Cudmore, L. (1986). The use of teacher-judgment measures in the identification of gifted pupils. *Teaching & Teacher Education, 2,* 181–196.

Kay, S. I. (in press). From novice to expert: A pilot study of students' perceptions of developing talent. In N. Colangelo & S. Assouline (Eds.), *Talent Development: Proceedings from the 1998 Henry B. and Jocelyn Wallace National Research Symposium on Talent Development.* Dayton, OH: Ohio Psychology Press.

Lacasse, L. (1990). *Étude comparative de la fidélité interjuges d'une grille de désignation par les pairs pour le dépistage des aptitudes et des talents aux niveaux primaire et secondaire.* [Comparative study of the inter-judge reliability of a peer nomination form for the screening of aptitudes and talents at the elementary and high school levels.] Unpublished master's thesis, Université du Québec à Montréal, Montréal, Canada.

Leblanc, F. (1998). *Évaluation psychométrique de deux grilles de désignations par les pairs pour le dépistage des talents.* [Psychometric evaluation of two peer nomination forms for the screening of talents.] Unpublished master's thesis, Université du Québec à Montréal, Montréal, Canada.

Marland, S. P. (1972). *Education of the gifted and talented: Report to the Congress of the United States by the U.S. Commissioner of Education.* Washington, DC: U.S. Government Printing Office.

Massé, L. (1992). *Analyse psychométrique des auto-désignations dans le dépistage des tal-*

References

ents par les pairs. [Psychometric analysis of self-nominations in relationship with the screening of talents by peers.] Unpublished master's thesis, Université du Québec à Montréal, Montréal, Canada.

Massé, L., & Gagné, F. (1996). Should self-nominations be allowed in peer nomination forms? *Gifted Child Quarterly, 40,* 24–30.

Pask-McCartney, C., & Salomone, P. R. (1988). Difficult cases in career counseling: III-The multipotential client. *The Career Development Quarterly, 36,* 231–240.

Pegnato, C. W., & Birch, J. W. (1959). Locating gifted children in junior high schools: A comparison of methods. *Exceptional Children, 25,* 300–304.

Silverman, L. K. (1993). Career counseling. In L. K. Silverman (Ed.), *Counseling the gifted and talented,* (pp. 215–238). Denver, CO: Love.

Tabachnick, B. G., & Fidell, L. S. (1989). *Using multivariate statistics* (2nd ed.). New York: Harper Collins.

Talbot, L. (1991). *Les dimensions des habiletés par le biais des désignations des pairs* [The dimensions of abilities from peer nominations]. Unpublished master's thesis, Université du Québec à Montréal, Montréal, Canada.

Terman, L. M. (1925). *Genetic studies of genius: Vol. 1. Mental and physical traits of a thousand gifted children.* Stanford, CA: Stanford University Press.

Appendix A

❊ ❊

Brief Description
of Gagné's Differentiated Model
of Giftedness and Talent (DMGT)

Gagné's Differentiated Model of Giftedness and Talent (DMGT) proposes a clear distinction between the concepts of giftedness and talent. The term GIFTEDNESS designates the possession and use of untrained and spontaneously expressed natural abilities (called aptitudes or gifts), in at least one ability domain, to a degree that places an individual at least among the top 10% of his or her age peers. By contrast, the term TALENT designates the superior mastery of systematically developed abilities (or skills) and knowledge in at least one field of human activity to a degree that places an individual within at least the upper 10% of age peers who are or have been active in that field or fields.

Gifts

The DMGT proposes five aptitude domains (see Figure 1): intellectual, creative, socioaffective, perceptual/motor, and "others." These natural abilities, whose development and level of expression is partially controlled by the individual's genetic endowment, can be observed in every task children are confronted with in the course of their schooling: For instance, the intellectual abilities needed to learn to read, speak a foreign language, or understand new mathematical concepts, the creative abilities needed to solve many different kinds of problems and produce original work in science, literature and art, the physical abilities involved in sport, music or woodwork, or the social abilities that children use daily in interactions with classmates, teachers, and parents. High aptitudes or gifts can be observed more easily and directly in young children because environmental influences and systematic learning have exerted their moderating influence in a limited way only. However, they still show themselves in older children and even in adults through the facility and speed with which individuals acquire new skills in any given field of human activity. The easier or faster the learning process, the greater the natural abilities. It is these high natural abilities that some laypersons call "talent" or, more appropriately, "natural talent."

Talents

As defined in the DMGT, talents progressively emerge from the transformation of these high aptitudes into the well-trained and systematically developed skills characteristic of a particular field of human activity or performance. These fields can be extremely diverse. Figure 1 shows some of the many talent fields relevant to school-aged youth. A given natural ability can express itself in many different ways, depending on the field of activity adopted by the individual. For example, dexterity, as a natural physical ability, can be modelled into the particular manual skills of a pianist, a painter, or a video-game player. Similarly, intelligence as a natural ability can be modelled into the scientific reasoning of a chemist, the game analysis of a chess player, or the strategic planning of an athlete.

Talent development

In this model, natural abilities or aptitudes act as the "raw material" or the constituent elements of talents. It follows from this relationship that talent necessarily implies the presence of

Figure 1
Gagné's Differentiated Model of Giftedness and Talent (DMGT)

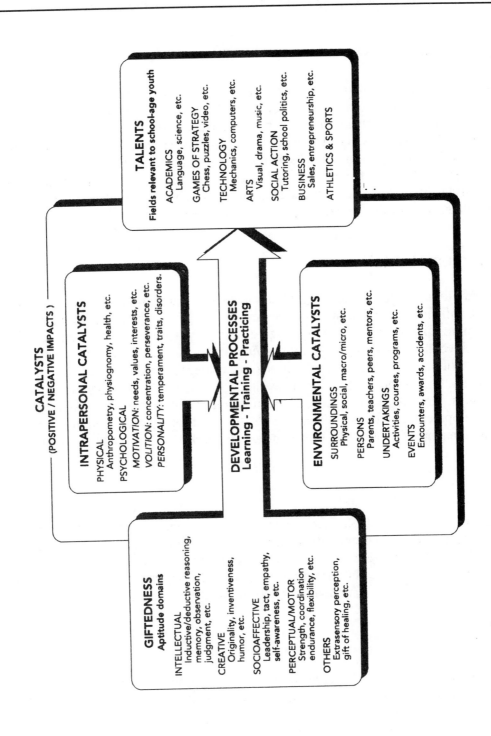

well above average natural abilities; one cannot be talented without first being gifted. The reverse is not true, however. It is possible for well above average natural abilities to remain simply as gifts, and not to be translated into talents, as is witnessed by the well-known phenomenon of academic underachievement among intellectually gifted children. The process of talent development manifests itself when the child or adolescent engages in systematic *learning, training, and practicing*; the higher the level of talent sought, the more intensive these three activities will be.

Intrapersonal catalysts

This process is facilitated (or hindered) by the action of two types of catalysts; *intrapersonal* and *environmental*. The intrapersonal catalysts are subdivided into physical and psychological factors, all of them under the partial influence of the genetic endowment. Among the psychological catalysts, motivation and volition play a crucial role in initiating the process of talent development, guiding it and sustaining it through obstacles, boredom, and occasional failure. Hereditary predispositions to behave in certain ways (temperament), as well as acquired styles of behavior (e.g., traits and disorders), also contribute significantly to support and stimulate, or slow down and even block, talent development.

Environmental catalysts

The environment manifests its significant impact in many different ways. The *surroundings* exert their influence both at a macroscopic level (e.g., geographic, demographic, sociological) and in a more microscopic framework (size of family, personality and parenting style of caregivers, socioeconomic status, and so forth). Many different *persons*, not only parents and teachers but also siblings and peers, may exert positive or negative influence on the process of talent development. Gifted education programs within or outside the school belong to the category of *undertakings*; they are a more systematic form of intervention to foster or hinder the process of talent development. Finally, significant *events* (the death of a parent, winning a prize or award, suffering a major accident or illness) can influence markedly the course of talent development.

Chance

Chance could be added as a fifth causal factor associated with the environment; but, strictly speaking, it is more appropriately a characteristic of some of the elements placed in any of the other four categories (e.g., the "chance" of being born in a particular family; the "chance" of the school in which the child is enrolled deciding to develop a program for gifted/talented students). Chance is also a major causal factor in the determination of the genetic endowment.

Prevalence

Any definition of normative concepts must specify how subjects differ from the norm and what it means in terms of the prevalence of the population subsumed under the label. In the

DMGT, the threshold for both the giftedness and talent concepts is placed at the 90th percentile (approximately 1.3 standard deviations above the mean); in other words, those who belong to approximately the top 10% of the relevant reference group in terms of ability (for giftedness) or achievement (for talent) may receive the relevant label.

Levels

It must be clearly noted, however, that this generous choice of threshold is counterbalanced by a recognition of levels or degrees of giftedness or talent. These comprise five groups. Within the top 10% of "basically" gifted or talented persons, the DMGT recognizes four progressively more selective subgroups. They are labeled "moderately" (top 1%), "highly" (top 1:1,000), "exceptionally" (top 1:10,000), and "extremely" (top 1:100,000). As in other fields of special education, the nature of the intervention program that a school develops for gifted or talented students should be influenced by the level of the student's giftedness or talent as well as the domains or fields in which it is sited.

Suggested Readings

Gagné, F. (1993). Constructs and models pertaining to exceptional human abilities. In K. A. Heller, F. J. Mönks & A. H. Passow (Eds.), *International Handbook of Research and Development of Giftedness and Talent* (pp. 63–85). Oxford: Pergamon Press.

Gagné, F. (1995). From giftedness to talent: A developmental model and its impact on the language of the field. *Roeper Review, 18,* 103–111.

Gagné, F. (1995). Hidden meanings of the "talent development" concept. *The Educational Forum, 59,* 350–362.

Gagné, F. (1998). A proposal for subcategories within the gifted or talented populations. *Gifted Child Quarterly, 42,* 87–95.

Appendix B

* *

**Schematic Description
of the 42 Items
in the Experimental Item Pool**

Intellectual aptitudes

ENCYCLOPEDIA: knows lots of things about all kinds of subjects, not just school subjects.
LIGHTNING: understands explanations quickly and often finds the right answers before others.
STRATEGIST: is very good at games of reasoning such as chess, checkers, Risk, Monopoly, etc.

Creative aptitudes

BRIGHT IDEA: has lots of imagination and lots of projects and suggestions for activities to do in class or in the school.
ORIGINAL: has new and different opinions or suggestions that no one else has thought of.

Socioaffective aptitudes

DIPLOMAT: knows how to make friends and talks easily with everyone, even adults or children she or he doesn't know.
CONFIDANT: knows how to listen, and does not repeat secrets that she or he receives; knows how to comfort other kids and make them feel better again.
GUARDIAN ANGEL: knows what is right and wrong, fair and unfair. A guardian angel gives us good advice to help us act the way we should.
CHEERLEADER: knows how to encourage others to do their best and not to give up when things are going badly.

Physical aptitudes

HARE: is always faster than others in physical activities (for example, when running, swimming, or riding a bicycle).
TIRELESS ONE: can play sports or games for a long time without getting out of breath or exhausted.
HERCULES: has very strong arms or legs and can lift very heavy objects.
GYMNAST: is good at physical exercises requiring rhythm, balance, flexibility, and coordination.
QUICK WRIST: is very good at games or sports requiring reflexes that are as quick as lightning (for example, video games, ping pong, magic tricks).

Interpersonal talents

LIFE OF THE PARTY: always has games or group activities to propose and makes parties lively, so that everyone has fun.
JUDGE: is very good at settling arguments between pupils and knows how to help people compromise and reach an agreement.
TEACHER: knows how to find the right words and examples to explain things that one didn't understand in class.
SPEAKER: expresses her or himself well and can talk about a subject in front of the class or other people without reading a text.
LEADER: directs others well and knows how to get people to listen and obey when she or he tells them what to do or how to do it.

Appendix B

SPOKESPERSON: is good at defending the class's point of view when it comes to obtaining permission to do something or changing a rule or a teacher's decision.

SALESPERSON: knows how to find the right arguments to persuade and convince others that her or his ideas are the best.

ADMINISTRATOR: works in a very orderly way. When there is a project to do, the administrator thinks of all the details, knows how to distribute the work and is never caught at the last minute.

BUSINESSMAN: has a talent for business and knows how to think up and organize an activity that will raise money.

Academic talents

GRAMMAR BOOK: knows grammar rules well and writes without spelling mistakes.

DICTIONARY: has a large vocabulary and uses unusual or complicated words correctly.

LINGUIST: learns to speak foreign languages quickly and easily.

GEOGRAPHER: knows a lot about different parts of the world and about the way people live in different countries.

SCIENTIST: knows a lot about science (for example, about plants, animals, chemicals, or planets).

CALCULATOR: is very quick with numbers and can easily solve complicated math problems.

Technical talents

MECHANIC: is very good at operating things such as VCRs, televisions, record players, etc. A mechanic can even repair simple machines.

PROGRAMMER: is very good with computers. A programmer can learn new programs alone and does not need to ask for help when a program is not working.

HANDYMAN: is very good at inventing original machines and at designing and building all kinds of things.

Artistic talents

WRITER: writes stories, poems, and short plays that are very imaginative and original.

CRAFTSPERSON: can make all sorts of pretty and original things with her or his hands: sculptures, masks, jewelry, knitting, pottery, etc.

ARTIST: can draw anything: objects, animals, or people. Some artists prefer to do paintings or watercolors, others prefer doing cartoons or comic strips.

COMEDIAN: makes everyone laugh with her or his jokes, imitations, or improvisations.

ACTOR: whom one would choose to play the main role in a film or a play.

DANCER: follows the rhythm of music well; her or his movements are easy and graceful.

MUSICIAN: plays a musical instrument very well.

SINGER: has a beautiful voice and sings in tune without any wrong notes.

[Underachievement]

SPARK: is very smart, but usually hides it by not studying and by getting bad grades.

FLICKERER: does very good work only when interested in a new subject.

Appendix C

Normative Percentages
for Various Categories
of Item, Subgroup, and MT Scores

Form A

Description	Score categories					
	0	1–9	10–19	20+	40+	60+
Items						
1. Encyclopedia	48	26	9	18	8	3
2. Handyman	32	34	14	20	4	2
3. Comedian	45	27	12	17	7	3
4. Programmer	35	34	14	18	4	2
5. Counselor/confidant	33	32	15	20	3	< 1
6. Lightning	48	25	10	17	7	4
7. Scientist	39	32	12	17	4	2
8. Stimulator/cheerleader	20	38	21	2i	2	1
9. Actor	33	30	16	20	4	1
10. Mechanic	38	31	14	17	4	1
11. Judge	25	34	20	20	2	< 1
12. Bright idea	28	33	19	20	3	1
Subgroups						
Academic (1, 6, 7, 12)	10	56	15	19	5	2
Mech/tech (2, 4, 10)	12	52	18	18	3	1
Arts-drama (3, 9)	22	42	15	21	4	1
Socioaffective (5, 8, 11)	9	47	25	19	1	< 1
MT score	3	52	25	21	1	< 1

Form B

Description	Score categories					
	0	1–9	10–19	20+	40+	60+
Items						
1. Hercules	54	23	7	16	7	3
2. Musician	48	25	9	18	7	3
3. Leader	35	32	14	19	4	< 1
4. Artist	44	27	12	16	7	3
5. Singer	42	32	12	14	2	1
6. Sociable/diplomat	23	33	21	23	2	< 1
7. Spokesperson	36	32	13	18	5	2
8. Tireless one	36	31	13	19	5	2
9. Craftsperson	29	34	18	19	3	< 1
10. Dancer	42	31	10	17	4	1
11. Speaker	39	30	11	20	6	1
12. Hare	40	28	13	19	7	3
Subgroups						
Physical	20	47	12	20	6	2
Music	18	50	12	20	3	1
Visual arts	21	43	18	18	5	1
Social influence	7	54	20	19	3	1
MT score B	3	51	25	21	< 1	--

Appendix D

❖ ❖

Reproducible Forms:
Data Sheet
Scoring Pad
Score Sheet: Form A
Score Sheet: Form B

TRACKING TALENTS

Data sheet

School: _____

Grade/Group: _____ Form: _____

Student's identification number (SIN)

Item	Pts	3	6	9	12	15	18	21	24	27	30	Teach.
1	3 2 1											— — —
2	3 2 1											— — —
3	3 2 1											— — —
4	3 2 1											— — —
5	3 2 1											— — —
6	3 2 1											— — —
7	3 2 1											— — —
8	3 2 1											— — —
9	3 2 1											— — —
10	3 2 1											— — —
11	3 2 1											— — —
12	3 2 1											— — —

Self-nomin.

TRACKING TALENTS

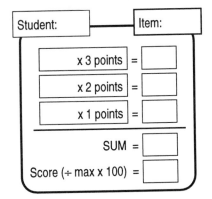

Scoring Pad

School: _____

Grade/Group: _____

MAX: [ ]

Student:		Item:	
	x 3 points	=	[ ]
	x 2 points	=	[ ]
	x 1 points	=	[ ]
	SUM	=	[ ]
	Score (÷ max x 100)	=	[ ]

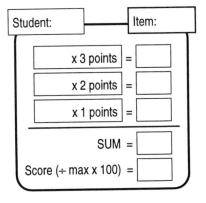

Student:		Item:	
	x 3 points	=	[ ]
	x 2 points	=	[ ]
	x 1 points	=	[ ]
	SUM	=	[ ]
	Score (÷ max x 100)	=	[ ]

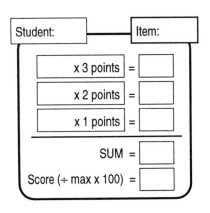

Student:		Item:	
	x 3 points	=	[ ]
	x 2 points	=	[ ]
	x 1 points	=	[ ]
	SUM	=	[ ]
	Score (÷ max x 100)	=	[ ]

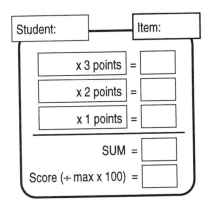

Student:		Item:	
	x 3 points	=	[ ]
	x 2 points	=	[ ]
	x 1 points	=	[ ]
	SUM	=	[ ]
	Score (÷ max x 100)	=	[ ]

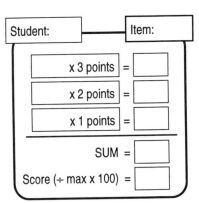

Student:		Item:	
	x 3 points	=	[ ]
	x 2 points	=	[ ]
	x 1 points	=	[ ]
	SUM	=	[ ]
	Score (÷ max x 100)	=	[ ]

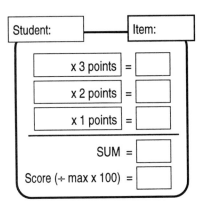

Student:		Item:	
	x 3 points	=	[ ]
	x 2 points	=	[ ]
	x 1 points	=	[ ]
	SUM	=	[ ]
	Score (÷ max x 100)	=	[ ]

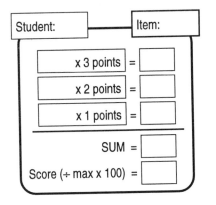

Student:		Item:	
	x 3 points	=	[ ]
	x 2 points	=	[ ]
	x 1 points	=	[ ]
	SUM	=	[ ]
	Score (÷ max x 100)	=	[ ]

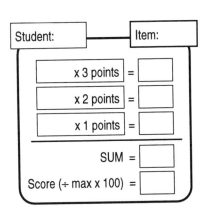

Student:		Item:	
	x 3 points	=	[ ]
	x 2 points	=	[ ]
	x 1 points	=	[ ]
	SUM	=	[ ]
	Score (÷ max x 100)	=	[ ]

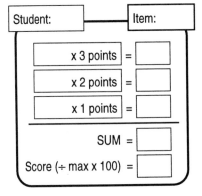

Student:		Item:	
	x 3 points	=	[ ]
	x 2 points	=	[ ]
	x 1 points	=	[ ]
	SUM	=	[ ]
	Score (÷ max x 100)	=	[ ]

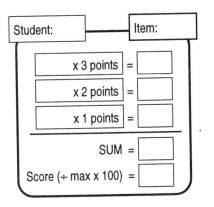

Student:		Item:	
	x 3 points	=	[ ]
	x 2 points	=	[ ]
	x 1 points	=	[ ]
	SUM	=	[ ]
	Score (÷ max x 100)	=	[ ]

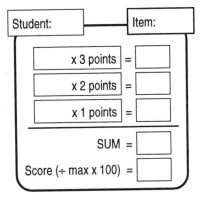

Student:		Item:	
	x 3 points	=	[ ]
	x 2 points	=	[ ]
	x 1 points	=	[ ]
	SUM	=	[ ]
	Score (÷ max x 100)	=	[ ]

Student:		Item:	
	x 3 points	=	[ ]
	x 2 points	=	[ ]
	x 1 points	=	[ ]
	SUM	=	[ ]
	Score (÷ max x 100)	=	[ ]

TRACKING TALENTS

Score Sheet: Form A

School: _____

Grade/Group: _____

MAX: [   ]

SIN	Name	Gender	Self-nominations	ACADEMIC					MECH-TECH				DRAMA			SOCIO-AFFECT				MT Score
				1 - Encyclopedia	6 - Lightning	7 - Scientist	12 - Bright Idea	Mean	2 - Handyman	4 - Programmer	10 - Mechanic	Mean	3 - Comedian	9 - Actor	Mean	5 - Counselor	8 - Stimulator	11 - Judge	Mean	
1		B ¦ G																		
2		B ¦ G																		
3		B ¦ G																		
4		B ¦ G																		
5		B ¦ G																		
6		B ¦ G																		
7		B ¦ G																		
8		B ¦ G																		
9		B ¦ G																		
10		B ¦ G																		
11		B ¦ G																		
12		B ¦ G																		
13		B ¦ G																		
14		B ¦ G																		
15		B ¦ G																		
16		B ¦ G																		
17		B ¦ G																		
18		B ¦ G																		
19		B ¦ G																		
20		B ¦ G																		
21		B ¦ G																		
22		B ¦ G																		
23		B ¦ G																		
24		B ¦ G																		
25		B ¦ G																		
26		B ¦ G																		
27		B ¦ G																		
28		B ¦ G																		
29		B ¦ G																		
30		B ¦ G																		

TRACKING TALENTS

Score Sheet: Form B

School: _____

Grade/Group: _____

MAX: _____

SIN	Name	Gender	Self-nominations	PHYSICAL				MUSIC				VISUAL			INTERPERSONAL					MT Score
				1 - Hercules	8 - Tireless One	12 - Hare	Mean	2 - Musician	5 - Singer	10 - Dancer	Mean	4 - Artist	9 - Craftsperson	Mean	3 - Leader	6 - Sociable	7 - Spokesperson	11 - Speaker	Mean	
1		B G																		
2		B G																		
3		B G																		
4		B G																		
5		B G																		
6		B G																		
7		B G																		
8		B G																		
9		B G																		
10		B G																		
11		B G																		
12		B G																		
13		B G																		
14		B G																		
15		B G																		
16		B G																		
17		B G																		
18		B G																		
19		B G																		
20		B G																		
21		B G																		
22		B G																		
23		B G																		
24		B G																		
25		B G																		
26		B G																		
27		B G																		
28		B G																		
29		B G																		
30		B G																		